P9-BTN-130

Chief Joseph of the Nez Perce Indians

Champion of Liberty

Chief Joseph of the Nez Perce Indians
Champion of Liberty

By Mary Virginia Fox

Consultant: Jay Miller, Ph.D.
D'Arcy McNickle Center for the History of the American Indian
The Newberry Library
Chicago, Illinois

 CHILDRENS PRESS®
CHICAGO

FRANKLIN PIERCE COLLEGE
LIBRARY
RINDGE, NEW HAMPSHIRE

Library of Congress Cataloging-in-Publication Data
Fox, Mary Virginia.
   Chief Joseph: champion of liberty/by Mary Virginia Fox.
   p. cm. — (People of distinction)
   Includes index.
   Summary: Relates the life story of the Nez Percé Indian chief who
led his people on a great trek to escape the injustices of the
American government.
   ISBN 0-516-03275-5
   1. Joseph, Nez Percé Chief, 1840-1904 — Juvenile literature. 2. Nez
Percé Indians — Biography — Juvenile literature. 3. Nez Percé
Indians — History — Juvenile literature. 4. Indians of North America —
Northwest, Pacific — History — Juvenile literature. (1. Joseph, Nez
Percé Chief, 1840-1904. 2. Nez Percé Indians — Biography. 3. Indians
of North America — Biography.) I. Title. II. Series.
E99.N5F69   1992   979'.004974 — dc20
                                                        91-35053
                                                            CIP
                                                             AC

CURR
E
99
.N5
F69
1992

Copyright 1992 by Childrens Press,® Inc.
All rights reserved. Published simultaneously in Canada.
Printed in the United States of America.
1 2 3 4 5 6 7 8 9 10 R 00 99 98 97 96 95 94 93 92

ACKNOWLEDGMENTS

Quotations used in this book come from: *Chief Joseph's Own Story* from the *North American Review,* April 1879; *Nez Perce Joseph* by O.O. Howard (Boston: Lee and Shepard Publishers, 1881); *The Flight of the Nez Perce* by Mark H. Brown (New York: G. P. Putnam's Sons, 1967); *War Chief Joseph* by Helen Addison Howard (Lincoln: University of Nebraska Press, 1964); and *"I Will Fight No More Forever"* by Merrill D. Beal (Seattle: University of Washington Press, 1973).

PICTURE ACKNOWLEDGMENTS

Courtesy Buffalo Bill Historical Center, Cody, Wyoming—56 (bottom)

Idaho State Historical Society—8, 52 (3 photos), 53 (top), 54 (bottom), 55 (2 photos), 57 (bottom), 58, 90 (top), 97

Montana Historical Society—10, 54 (top left and right), 90 (bottom)

National Park Service, Nez Perce National Historic Park—2 Neg. No. 2337

Oregon Historical Society—53 (bottom) Neg. No. #002939-0302P050, 56 (top) Neg. No. #56265 F1132A, 57 (top) Neg. No. ORHI 21694, 98 Neg. No. ORHI52504-9999Y987

Smithsonian Institution—4 Neg. No. 2916-A

Cover illustration by Len W. Meents

Project Editor: Mary Reidy
Designer: Karen A. Yops

Table of Contents

Chief Joseph in 1877

Chapter 1

FAREWELL TO THE VALLEY OF WINDING WATERS

The first rays of sun had just burst over the mountains sheltering the Valley of Winding Waters in the northeast corner of what was called the Oregon Territory. There had been little sleep that night in the lodges that sheltered families of the Nez Perce Indians living there. Old and young warriors sat up until dawn debating whether they should leave their hunting grounds behind and move two weeks' journey north to the Nez Perce Reservation across the Salmon River.

There had been much talk: talk about the wrongs they had suffered because of white people, talk about the strength of the whites' army, and talk about the promises that the whites had made and broken in the past. There had been other treaties where tribes of Nez Perce had given up land in exchange for a guarantee that there would be no more settlers past the boundary of the Bitterroot Mountains. As soon as the treaties had been signed, they had been broken. There seemed to be no end to the whites' greed for land.

With more settlers there came more soldiers—soldiers equipped with guns and cannons. Forts had been built on the Indians' hunting grounds. Were the Nez Perce always to give in to these trespassers, many warriors asked?

Young Joseph, chief of the Wal-lam-wat-kin band of the Nez Perce, knew how foolish it was of the whites to think anyone could own the land, but he urged his people to consider the death and suffering they would endure if they fought the white soldiers. One battle would surely not settle the differences. More soldiers would be added to the fight. The Nez Perce would have to defend themselves continually. The man who spoke for the whites was a soldier, General Howard. He had told them that there was an even greater leader, known as President Rutherford B. Hayes, who had made rules all must follow. He told Joseph's band that they would have to leave the Valley of Winding Waters, either peacefully or by force.

They had one month to resettle. By the whites' calendar it was May 15, 1877. By the Indians' sense of time, it was the height of the spring floods in the mountains. They would have to ford more than one raging river. With women and children and herds of cattle and horses, this would be very difficult.

There were many young braves who were ready to fight for their freedom. Joseph warned them that if force were to be used to keep their tribe together, it would be he who would be aiming a gun, not the whites. It was now time to move. There was much to be done in preparation.

Herders were sent to the hills to round up their cattle and horses. Lodge poles had to come down and buffalo robes and rush matting had to be bundled and tied onto pack horses. Dried salmon, venison, and buffalo meat were tied in sacks.

Berries, fruits, and nuts that had been saved from the winter's hoard were now put in pouches and added to the baggage.

Most of the Nez Perce would be making the trip on fine ponies, but there were not enough tame mounts for everyone. It would be a slow journey. Chief Joseph's wife was about to have a baby. She would not be able to keep up with a war party, but war was not what they were expecting.

It was with grieving hearts that the plans were carried out. By week's end the band of some six hundred Indians had assembled for the trek that would take them from the Valley of Winding Waters forever. To the west jagged ridges with forested slopes girdled the valley. To the south and east lofty peaks rose thousands of feet into the sky, snowfields still deep at their crests. Bunch grass and sage carpeted the valley floor, broken by meandering streams where the first run of blueback salmon were fighting their way to the spawning grounds. Life had been good in this valley. It was a land of plenty.

What was to come next was still a question. Chief Joseph hoped with all his heart that his decision to leave their ancestral home would bring peace. Other leaders might have been called cowards, but not Joseph. He had proven his bravery many times. No one ever judged Joseph less than a compassionate and wise leader.

On the third day the band reached the banks of the Snake River. The roar of water drowned the sound of their voices. The snowmelt was at its peak. The current dashing against large boulders close to shore sent spray spewing into the gray sky. Joseph gave the order to prepare for the crossing. If they waited longer they would not reach the reservation in time to meet General Howard's "limit for my patience"—the words he had used.

Joseph watched as they unrolled their rafts. The baggage was unroped from the carrier ponies. Women and children stood in groups and waited their turn for the crossing. Joseph's wife, heavy with child, seated herself confidently at the forward edge of the first raft. Four of the strongest warriors, mounted on four horses, each took hold of a corner of the raft and swam their cargo across the quarter mile of treacherous, dragging current. Water boiled up and over the sides of the raft, but on the first trip all arrived safely on the other side. Many trips still had to be made.

As soon as the old and young had made the crossing, it was time to swim the livestock across. The sky had darkened. Suddenly blinding rain added to their misery. Even the best-schooled hunting horses turned skittish as they were forced into the river. Cattle had to be roped and dragged to the water's edge. Many were swept to a quick death.

Joseph, who had remained on the near shore, ordered the men who were still with him to stop herding the animals into the water. He told those who had not yet made the crossing to remain where they were until the flood stage of the river subsided. He left a small number of warriors to guard the animals and keep them from roaming off. Surely General Howard would understand if not all arrived at the reservation by the deadline, he thought. Only then did he plunge into the chill waters to join the others.

They did not camp until late that day. There was little time to warm themselves over fires, but they assembled before dawn the following morning. They had to cross another ford at the Salmon River, a tributary of the Snake. This time the current was not as swift. No more animals were lost, but some of their food supply was washed from the rafts.

A few miles from there they joined the camp of Chief White Bird's band in Rocky Canyon, eight miles west of the white settlement of Grangeville. Eleven days remained before their time limit was up, but now there seemed to be no rush. They were close to the southwest boundary of the Lapwai Reservation. Other groups joined them. There was a festive air as friends and relatives were reunited.

Only when Tuhulhutsut, chief of the Pikunanmu tribe of Nez Perce, and his people arrived was there dissent. Tuhulhutsut was one of the leading *tewats*, "medicine men," of the Dreamer faith, who had never given up his beliefs in the sanctity of the spirits of nature. He spurned his people who had submitted to Christian baptism. He had come to preach his own gospel, that "The earth is the mother of life," and the white settlers who had come to farm the soil were ripping the skin of the very spirit who gave them life.

His followers who lived along the Snake River were small in numbers, but Tuhulhutsut was a passionate orator, and any new voice against white power was greeted with enthusiasm by those who opposed Joseph's voice of peace.

Tuhulhutsut's words were spoken in anger. There was nothing in his beliefs, he told them, that taught that whites could dictate where each race should live. That was the right of the Spirit Chief.

There were shouts of approval. Now against the inflamed feelings of his own people, Chief Joseph once more pleaded for peace and pointed to the folly of taking the warpath. Chief White Bird, who at one time had been ready to band together with Joseph's people, now stated clearly that he was ready to prepare for war.

While discontent was running high, another blow against peace was delivered. The herders, who had been left to guard the horses and cattle on the banks of the Snake River, arrived to say that a band of whites had ridden down on the herd and stampeded them deliberately.

Chief Joseph had to use all his power to keep order. He pointed out that the lawbreakers were not soldiers, and that when the Nez Perce reached the reservation, their herds of animals would be protected. The white people's laws would be their laws. But not everyone believed his words.

The young warrior named Walaitits shouted boldly that he had seen white justice. His father had been killed by a white man, Larry Ott, in an unprovoked quarrel over land. Ott had admitted his crime but had never been punished. Several of his friends taunted Walaitits that he was a coward not to have sought revenge.

It took all of Joseph's skill to stop a war party from being formed immediately. Only the combined voices of some of the older warriors, joining with his, held the group together. Convinced that he had won his point, Chief Joseph left the council to butcher some of his cattle for his family. Too many supplies had already been lost on the first leg of their journey.

While Joseph was gone from camp, someone distributed an ample supply of whiskey. Not all had acquired a taste for the "fire water," but two young warriors, Isapsis-ilpilp and Um-til-ilp-cown, offered to join Walaitits in seeking revenge. All three were members of White Bird's band.

The father of Isapsis-ilpilp rode after his son and tried to persuade him to return to the camp. It was not natural for a son to rebel against the orders of his father, but Isapsis-ilpilp was now drunk and ready for bloodletting.

The rebels did not find Larry Ott at his cabin, but twenty miles from Fort Lapwai along the Slate Creek, the three came upon the homestead of Richard Divine, an old retired sailor, living alone. There wasn't much of a struggle, but the murder of a white man fired their feelings of bravery and lust for more conquests.

Later in the day, June 13, 1877, they killed three other settlers, Robert Bland, Henry Elfers, and Henry Beckroge, who were working in their fields. They left Mrs. Elfers and her three children unharmed, but took guns and ammunition and fresh horses. They then rode down the Salmon River trail where they met and fired upon another settler, Samuel Benedict, wounding him in both legs.

The young men galloped back toward White Bird's camp on the afternoon of June 14. Aflame with reckless courage, they rode through the village shouting, "Now you will have to go to war! See! Walaitits has killed men and stolen horses! Now the soldiers will come after us! Prepare for war! Prepare for war!"

Suddenly pent up emotions that had been smoldering burst forth. White Bird decided to join the young rebels and the tewats. The tewats had been haranguing for a war to revenge the spirits of ancestors whose burial grounds were being desecrated by whites. It was the beginning of a bloody war that was to take many lives and would split two races with hatred and fear. When Chief Joseph returned to the camp, there was no way he could change the course of history.

Chapter 2

IN THE BEGINNING

The Nimipu, the tribal name of the Nez Perce, lived in many places. They had learned to value horses that had first been brought to the Southwest by early settlers, but had since run wild across fenceless plains. Their hunting and fishing grounds extended many days' travel in all directions. They roamed the grassy plateaus and valleys during the spring, summer, and fall seeking pasture for their livestock. Their warrior hunters migrated east each year across the Bitterroot Mountains to kill buffalo. Others made camp along the Salmon River, which ran into the Snake River, to harvest fish. In the winter they built their lodges in the sheltered valleys of the Wallowa Range in what is now the state of Oregon.

The Nimipu seldom went hungry. They smoked the meat of deer (venison), buffalo, and salmon to be used in all seasons. They dug up the camas and kouse roots that grew in the grasslands and ground them into a flour that was used to thicken their stews and to make a flat-crusted bread. They harvested berries, nuts, and small fruits that grew along their yearly paths of migration.

They were a healthy, strong group of people, taller than most of their neighbors and with a record of remarkable longevity for a race that the whites mistakenly called primitive. They were a proud and peace-loving people, friends with the Flatheads, the Cayuse, and the Abasaroka (Crows). Their legend of the birth of their people was told many times by the elders of the tribe so that these lessons could be passed on to the young.

It was said that a huge monster from the sea, the great Iltswetsix, roamed the Kamiah Valley in northern Idaho. He was a terrible creature that started to devour all the animals of the land. It was not until clever Coyote, or Spi-li-yai, tested his strength against the monster that the land was saved.

Coyote tied himself down with a wild grapevine and then dared the monster to try to pull him from the safety of his den. Iltswetsix sucked a blast of air into his mighty lungs, breaking the rope that tied Coyote, drawing the prey deep into his stomach. But clever Coyote had expected this to happen, so he took out a knife he had hidden on his body and killed the monster. He then carved his way out of the sea demon's stomach.

Coyote was trying to decide what to do with the monster's body when Fox came by and suggested that they cut it up to make people. So from the head they made the Flathead Indians and from the feet the Blackfoot tribe. From each part they made a different nation of Indians. Finally only the heart remained. As Coyote squeezed it, blood dripped to the ground, and from these drops the Nez Perce people sprang up. They were taller, nobler, and wiser than all the rest. These were the Nimipu. So that no one would forget this wonderful deed, the Spirit Chief, who rules over all, turned the heart into a large stone that still can be seen in the Kamiah Valley.

The first white the Nimipus ever saw was William Clark, who had set out on an expedition with Meriwether Lewis to cross the North American continent and to report to President Thomas Jefferson what was to be found in the far northwest. The date was recorded in Clark's journal as September 20, 1805. It was a peaceful meeting.

The expedition had run low on food; so, while Lewis and the main body of explorers were crossing the Bitterroot Mountains, Clark took six hunters and hurried ahead to forage for game. They came upon a small camp of Indians near the western end of the Lolo Trail that snaked through the Bitterroot Mountains. The women were busy digging camas roots in what is now called the Wieppe Prairie. The two groups exchanged signs of friendship. The white leader gave the Indians a bronze disk with curious symbols. The Indians gave bundles of food.

When Lewis and Clark again joined forces, it was decided to leave their horses in the care of the Indians, one of whom was the son of Chief Twisted Hair. The rest of the expedition's journey was to be made by boat all the way to the Pacific. When they returned several months later, their horses were well cared for and waiting for them.

Lewis and Clark recorded many facts of interest about this tribe. They were lighter skinned than any Indians they had thus far contacted. They were tall and muscular, but graceful in their movements. Clark noted that each family unit or band had a permanent campsite in the narrow valleys along the Clearwater, Snake, and Salmon rivers. Here the Indians had permanent dwellings made of logs and hide that they called *lodges*. Near the rapids where they had fishing camps, they had smaller, flattopped lodges walled with rush matting that served both as shelters and a place to dry fish. When digging camas and kouse on the prairie, small temporary shelters made of bark and brush were used. The expedition members also noted that the Indians had large herds of horses, and the men possessed knowledge of breeding and health care for their animals.

Soon after Clark and Lewis reported on their findings, fur traders and trappers followed the same trails. The War of 1812 put a halt to much serious exploration by Americans, but officials of the Hudson Bay Company in Canada were the next to come across these peaceful Indians. The French Canadians immediately gave another name to these hardy, healthy native Americans. They called them Nez Perce, meaning "pierced nose," because some of them wore a thin shell through their noses. Not many clung to this custom, but it was a name easily pronounced by the French, and it came to be the term used by all whites for the handsome Nimipu Indians.

The Nez Perce were pleased to trade with the whites for useful articles: axes, flint, and iron kettles. A steady stream of white people were already pouring in from the east along the newly opened Oregon Trail. The Nez Perce became experts at horse trading. The tired and hungry work animals that had come this far from the east were often traded for fresh Indian ponies. In time the rested eastern stock grew fat and healthy on ample forage and were added to the breeding stock of the Nez Perce.

The Indians began to accept the idea that whites were in some way superior. Their spirit medicine must be strong to give them such strange powerful weapons as guns. Because the Indians' medicine represented their religion, they sought the whites' superior power through the God the white people worshiped.

In 1831 a small group of Flatheads and Nez Perce Indians started for St. Louis from their hunting grounds on the head-waters of the Missouri River. Their mission was to get some-one to come west with them to teach them the whites' "spirit laws." Only one warrior, Rabbit Skin Leggins, lived to return the next year; but this request from the land of "savages," as the whites called the tribes they had never met, changed the thoughts of several church groups. Here were people begging to be Christianized. It was a golden opportunity to spread the Gospel, but it was not until 1836 that the Christian church came to the Nez Perce.

Henry Spalding and his wife Elisa set up a Presbyterian mission at the mouth of Lapwai Creek as it entered Clearwater River, in what is now northern Idaho. The name Lapwai meant "Place Where the Butterfly Dwells." Not only was it a fine-sounding name, but its location was close to the spot where the Indians gathered to conduct business at the trapper trading post.

About the same time Father DeSmet established Saint Mary's Mission among the Flatheads in the Bitterroot Valley. It was puzzling to Indians that white people should have more than one religion, but there were more than enough converts to go around.

Chief Tu-eka-kas of the Nez Perce visited the Presbyterian mission and listened to the words of the preacher. He told Spalding that he wanted his people to learn the "white man's book" and the many useful things the strangers could teach the Indians.

Besides teaching the "spirit law," Spalding also taught the Indians how to till the soil and how to raise crops of wheat, corn, potatoes, and other foods. Spalding also introduced cattle, sheep, and hogs to the herds of horses and ponies and packs of dogs. Spalding's wife opened a mission school to teach the youngsters the elementary essentials of reading, writing, arithmetic, and English.

Chief Tu-eka-kas and Chief Twisted Hair were Spalding's first true converts. Tu-eka-kas took the name of Joseph and

Twisted Hair became known as Timothy. On November 17, 1839 the missionary proceeded to remarry Joseph and his wife with the recitation of Christian scripture. They had already pledged a native bond.

Chief Joseph became devoutly religious and used his influence among his people to spread the church Gospel. He guaranteed that he would assist in the responsibility of disciplining his people so that they would live honest and peaceful lives.

All seemed to be working well toward peaceful coexistence. Then the white government called for a meeting. They said that there should be a formal agreement that the Indians would abide by the whites' law. In actuality the Indians of the Nez Perce tribe were more law abiding than the trappers and miners who frequently went on drunken sprees, destroying property and taking lives.

In December 1842 the scattered bands comprising the Nez Perce nation held a council at Lapwai with Dr. Elijah White, subagent of Indian Affairs west of the Rocky Mountains, and four other representatives of the white community, including one official of the Hudson Bay Trading Company, for the purpose of proposing a system of criminal laws. The Indians agreed by acclamation.

White then suggested that they elect a head chief over all bands of the Nez Perce nation. This could not be done because it was in direct violation of the Nez Perce tribal customs. There had never been a rule by majority, even within the various bands. Members of each group voluntarily followed the counsel of their chief, who was assisted by various minor chiefs or headmen under him, and by medicine men who interpreted spiritual matters. But anyone could disagree with the decisions of the main group and still be considered a member of the band. This was contrary to the white people's way of thinking and never taken into consideration during the long hassles over treaties that were to follow.

At this time the Indians trusted the whites. A few Nez Perce were already learning to write their own language from the grammar Spalding had composed. Some could read the Gospel of Saint Matthew, which Spalding had translated into the Indians' native tongue. Most were learning words of English to communicate with the waves of whites moving west.

In 1845 Spalding baptized Chief Joseph's eldest son, then five years old, also giving him the name of Joseph. So from then on, to avoid confusion, the father was known as the Older Joseph and the son as Young Joseph.

Young Joseph's brother, Ollokot, was only two years younger than his brother. The two were always close. They looked so much alike that they were often mistaken for twins. For a while both boys attended the mission day school. They were not old enough to learn to read and write much English, but they acquired a certain respect for the white people's ways, at least the ways that were being taught from the Holy Bible.

A break in the peaceful cooperation between the whites,

who were beginning to follow the Spaldings into the Northwest Territory, and the Indians, who far outnumbered them, came in the fall of 1847. One hundred twenty miles to the south and west of the Spalding mission, another churchman, Dr. Marcus Whitman, had settled in territory dominated by Cayuse Indians. Whitman and his wife ministered to the health as well as the spiritual needs of their neighbors.

However, whites often brought their own ills as well as cures. There was an outbreak of measles among the tribes of the Cayuse, something they had never experienced before.

In the minds of some Indians, it was a curse meant to wipe out the red man. With savage treachery, yet with simple logic, the solution was to kill the whites before more Indian families died. On November 29, 1847 a band of Cayuse killed Doctor Whitman, his wife, and thirteen others at the mission. They burned buildings and took other women and children prisoner.

Spalding had just left the scene hours before, having ridden to Walla Walla to consult with Doctor Whitman. When he learned of the massacre, he hurried back to his own home to protect his family. Fearing that the northwestern Indians would start an all-out war, he asked his Nez Perce friends for an escort to the nearest fort manned by United States soldiers. Forty Nez Perce warriors volunteered to guide him to safety, to the white settlement at The Dalles in Oregon.

Even though the Nez Perce of Old Joseph's and Timothy's band were deserted by their preacher, they continued to practice their faith, and conducted religious services every Sunday. However, a few renegade Nez Perce looted the Spalding home at Lapwai. When the Reverend Spalding returned for a brief visit several months later, Old Joseph was held responsible for the actions. This brought on a serious breach in the friendly relations between Spalding and the Indian chief. It was about this time that Joseph took back his given name, Tu-eka-kas, and left the vicinity of Lapwai to return to the Wallowa Valley.

Soon after the Whitman massacre, several troops of United States cavalry were sent into the region to capture the Indians who had done the killing. They suspected that the Nez Perce had helped the guilty parties escape. For a while it seemed possible that the Nez Perce would be drawn into a war with the soldiers, but a meeting of whites and Indians took place in March 1848. Two hundred fifty warriors, led by Tu-eka-kas, approached the council grounds. The chief carried an American flag and a copy of the Bible Spalding had given him. General Palmer, the Indian superintendent of Oregon, was favorably impressed by the attitude of the Nez Perce, and hostilities were averted—at least for the time being.

Chapter 3

DIFFERENT WAYS

Although Young Joseph and his brother Ollokot were not brought up in a Christian church, moral lessons of behavior were strict. When he was older Joseph frequently spoke of the wise counsel given him by his father.

"Our fathers gave us many laws, which they had learned from their fathers. These laws were good. They told us to treat all men as they treated us; that we should never be the first to break a bargain; that it was a disgrace to tell a lie; that we should speak only the truth; that it was a shame for one man to take from another his wife, or his property without paying for it. We were taught to believe that the Great Spirit sees and hears everything, and that he never forgets; that hereafter he will give every man a spirit-home according to his desserts: if he has been a good man, he will have a good home; if he has been a bad man, he will have a bad home. This I believe, and all my people believe the same."

It was a creed that combined the lessons taught by past generations of Nez Perce with what had been learned from the Reverend Henry Spalding's missionary teaching. The only Indian custom frowned upon by the Christian church was polygamy—having more than one wife. The Nez Perce men felt an obligation to provide food for all women because women were not allowed to join the hunt. If a woman was left a widow, she usually married her next of kin or whomever was willing to take on added responsibilities. Tu-eka-kas had two wives. Joseph had six brothers and sisters, but Ollokot would always be his closest confidant and the one to whom he turned for advice.

Both boys were taught the skills of hunting, and how to survive in all kinds of weather. They learned to watch for the roots of plants that provided food and medicine. But the greatest lessons for every child, boys and girls alike, were those learned from the Great Spirit above.

When Young Joseph was ten years old he took part in a ceremony that was to mark him as an adult. Without food or clothing he was told to leave the camp and to prepare to hold communion with the spirits of nature that were all around him. He was told that if he sincerely asked for guidance, he would be rewarded. His spirit name would be given him. If not, the men of the tribe would give him a foolish name, one he would be ashamed of.

Sometime during his days of solitude, a vision did appear to Joseph, but it was to be a vision only he and the medicine man would know how to interpret.

When Joseph returned to the lodge of his family, all was in readiness for the ceremony. Two fires blazed in the dance tent. One warrior after another had his turn acting out a part of the history of the tribe. There were chants and songs. When Young Joseph's turn came he sang the mystic words that the Spirit Chief had taught him when he was in a trance in the wilderness. He had been blessed with the name Hin-mut-too-yah-lat-kekht, meaning "Thunder-Rolling-in-the-Mountains." It was a good sign. It meant that Joseph had been offered the protection of one of the most powerful beings in nature.

Young Joseph would need that protection because already the basis for dissatisfaction and war was taking place. His father was deeply troubled. Someday Young Joseph might have to assume some of these worries.

Diplomats in Washington and London were making decisions that would affect the destiny of the Nez Perce Indians. All of the region then known as Oregon country, now comprising the states of Washington and Oregon, Idaho, western Montana, and Wyoming, was claimed by the United States by right of discovery. The international border was settled peacefully by treaty between Britain and the United States on June 15, 1846. The boundary was drawn along the forty-ninth parallel of geographic latitude. With the stroke of a pen, the lands of Tu-eka-kas's band were placed under the rule of a stranger, without the old chief's consent or knowledge.

Two years later, in 1848, the Territory of Oregon was established; a new governor was inaugurated on March 3, 1849. Now that the wilderness had been opened to settlers from the east, more government officials were appointed to enforce more complicated laws that were supposed to bring peace— but peace for whom? Still the emigrants kept coming. There were enough people living in the area for the United States to draw more lines on a map, establishing the Territory of Washington out of the old Oregon Territory. It was hard for the Indians to imagine that there were so many white people on the earth.

The newly appointed governor of the Territory of Oregon, Isaac Stevens, had the military rank of major. He also was head of the railroad survey and superintendent of Washington Indian affairs. He could see that there were bound to be arguments between the Indians and the pioneers who were pouring into the Columbia River basin. Already there had been skirmishes between whites and the Cayuse, Klickitat, and Yakima tribes. If they were joined by the largest and most powerful Indian nation, the Nez Perce, there would be more trouble. The only solution seemed to be to separate the two races—to put the Indians on reservations, and keep the whites out of their territory.

With this in mind Stevens sent his representative, James Doty, to all Columbia River chiefs, calling for a council to settle the problem. Chief Kamiakin of the Yakimas chose Walla, the ancient council ground of the tribes, as the meeting place. Tu-eka-kas, Joseph's father, was one of the principal chiefs to accept the call, and he brought with him his two eldest sons, Joseph and Ollokot.

Joseph remembered the events of the council well. The Nez Perce were the first to assemble, although they did not arrive until four days after the time appointed because of spring floods. Next came the Cayuses, then the Walla Wallas, the Umatillas, and the Yakimas. Five thousand Indians assembled, making it the largest peaceful gathering of the tribes in their history.

Major Isaac Stevens, then thirty-six years of age, represented the United States government as governor of the territory. With him was his thirteen-year-old-son, Hazard, as proof that the white people meant no ambush. Four other minor officials of the territory and six interpreters who could speak in several Indian dialects, and two Catholic missionaries, Fathers Chirause and Pandosy, attended the council. They were guarded, in ceremony only, by forty-seven cavalrymen under Lieutenant Archibald Gracie.

As the different tribes arrived, their buffalo hide tipis and mat lodges were set up along the banks of Mill Creek. It was a gathering as large as most cities in the west. Campfires gave a blue haze to the otherwise clear air.

To impress the white officials the Nez Perce tribes, the largest group, prepared themselves carefully for the opening ceremonies. They rubbed their leather buckskins with chalk to give them a luminous cast in the sun. Their faces and the hides of their ponies were streaked with yellow and crimson. The men's hair was carefully braided and tied with colored strings. On their legs and feet they wore their best beaded moccasins. The older warriors wore their brightly colored plumed war bonnets. A thousand younger men, naked except for breechcloths, were mounted on their strongest ponies.

The women who had come with their men were not out-done. Colorful blanket shawls were tied over their shoulders. Their fringed buckskin dresses were painted and beaded in lavish color. Their high-topped moccasins reached their knees. These Nez Perce Indians of the great northwest were coming as equals.

Joseph remembered the pride he had felt as the horsemen galloped two abreast toward the mound where the governor's party stood in review. The warriors were armed with shields, lances, knives, and guns. This time their war cries were meant only to impress.

For two days Major Stevens tried to explain in detail the terms of the treaty the whites offered. At first he proposed two reservations—one in the country of the Nez Perce and the other in Yakima territory. In return for the Indians' peaceful move to the reservation, the treaties guaranteed that no whites would be allowed to trespass on land that was to be the Indians' new home. There would be no more disputes about butchered livestock. There would be no killing. The whites' laws were to protect them. These were provisions Tu-eka-kas favored. There were other provisions that seemed useless.

The United States government would build schools and

churches and sawmills and gristmills—things for which the Indians had had no need before, so why now? A few chiefs were to be paid five hundred dollars a year, but no one explained what they were to do with their money in a society that did not use money. Joseph's father knew all too well that it would be impossible to change their way of life so fast.

The Nez Perce chief named Lawyer signed the treaty for his people. There were other tribes, too, who were persuaded that peace was worth any compromise. Gifts were distributed by the whites to the Indians who signed the treaty, but they were small gifts for what was to be given in return.

Years later it was said Tu-eka-kas signed as well, but Joseph remembered his father's words.

"Why do you ask me to sign away my country? It is your business to talk to us about spirit matters, and not to talk to us about parting with our land. I will not sign your paper," he said, "you go where you please, so do I; you are not a child, I am no child; I can think for myself. No man can think for me. I have no other home than this. I will not give it up to any man. My people would have no home. Take away your paper. I will not touch it with my hand."

On June 8 Stevens made concessions to certain tribes designating the reservation land of the Umatillas, Cayuses, and Walla Wallas to be the site of their present hunting grounds and fishing streams. They would not be forced to move to strange ground. This was not to be true for the Nez Perce. The

Valley of the Winding Waters was to be opened to settlers.

Just as Stevens thought he had appeased the dissatisfied chiefs, a small party of Nez Perce warriors rode into the council grounds. The leader was old Chief Looking Glass, who had just returned from a three-year buffalo hunt on the plains.

He delivered a fiery speech. "My people, what have you done? While I was gone, you have sold my country. I have come home, and there is not left for me a place on which to pitch my lodge. Go home to your lodges. I will talk to you."

The conference was about to end with no decision, but again Lawyer took the lead. By vote of the majority, his claims to be head chief were upheld. On June 11 he signed a treaty that was forever to split the people of the Nez Perce tribe.

Others, particularly Peu-peu-mox-mox of the Walla Wallas, did not trust the whites and spoke against the treaty. Chief Lawyer went to Governor Stevens and told him that there were bands of Indians already plotting the murder of the white troops. Lawyer offered to be the intermediary. To show his loyalty Lawyer told Stevens he would pitch his lodge in the midst of the soldiers' camp. This would show the renegade Indians that the white people were under the protection of Nez Perce warriors.

Peace was restored, but Stevens began to believe that Lawyer was making up the threat of a plot to further his own reputation as a loyal and trusted friend who should be rewarded further.

The plot had indeed been brewing, and during the next two years there was bitter fighting to the north. The Indians found plenty of cause to be angry with the hordes of white miners who flocked into the northwest. The final act that started what was to be called the Treaty War or Stevens War was the murder of A.J. Bolton, the special agent for the Yakimas. He had tried to be fair with the Indians, but there was no way he could control the settlers who were breaking treaty rights.

His job was a difficult one. Congress, by the Donation Acts, urged Americans to settle the land that was now being opened up for "improvement." White settlers were encouraged to stake claims on land that really belonged to the Indians by treaty. The wording of the treaty clearly promised the Indians that no whites would be permitted to build on Indian land, graze animals on the land, or fish the rivers that ran through the land.

Bolton's murder was meant to send a message from the Indians to the white chiefs in the East that they would not stand for any more injustice, but his death only aroused the settlers to organize a volunteer force and to ask for military protection. Outright war broke out around Puget Sound in the territory of Washington and soon spread to all the smaller tribes in the northwest. The battles occurred in the late 1850s.

So far no large migrations of settlers had reached the lands of the Nez Perce. They still hoped they could live in harmony with the whites. No one wanted bloodshed. But only the Nez

Perce remained faithful to their pledge of peace.

The Indian rebellion was not completely suppressed until 1858 because of lack of coordination among the white troops.

Colonel George Wright brought an end to the skirmishes. His main aim was to retain the friendship of the Nez Perce and the smaller tribes of the area by guaranteeing that white soldiers would come to the defense of any tribe attacked by a hostile tribe. A company of thirty Nez Perce warriors was outfitted in army uniforms to help keep the peace.

But it was a risky peace. The Indians had reason to doubt the promises of the whites. Congress had yet to ratify the treaty that Stevens had so painstakingly drawn up.

Young Joseph's later criticism of the whites' government was well taken. "The white people have too many chiefs. They do not understand each other. They do not all talk alike."

Chapter 4

THE YOUNG CHIEF

In 1860 an Indian trader named Elias D. Pierce managed to slip onto the Nez Perce reservation where he found traces of gold. By December he and thirty-three other white prospectors had set up camp along the Oro Fino Creek. Indian Agent A.J. Cain could see the clouds of war gathering. He hoped to work out a compromise with the Indians.

The white people's solution always meant putting something down in writing. A legal document was drawn up permitting mining operations on Indian territory lying north of the Snake and Clearwater rivers in exchange for a modest payment of cash. Again it was promised that no whites would be permitted to build on Indian land. This was to be enforced by a military regiment posted on the reservation to preserve the peace of the country. Yet their very presence was felt by the Nez Perce to be an encroachment of Indian rights.

These articles of agreement were signed by Lawyer, who was recognized by the white negotiators as head chief of the Nez Perce nation.

By the time of the signing some three hundred miners had already set up claims along the Oro Fino Creek, and two months later two towns had been established, named Perce and Slaterville. By the first of June a steamboat had made its way up the Clearwater just above its junction with the Snake. Thus Lewiston was established in direct violation of the treaty. City lots were measured off and sold to the highest bidder.

Indian Agent Charles Hutchins, who had recently been appointed to his job, did his best to stop the flood of settlers and squatters, but "No Trespassing" signs were torn down and used as firewood.

Lawlessness quickly became a major problem, and by the spring of 1862 it was reported that about fifteen thousand people, mostly gold miners, had already spread across the Nez Perce reservation in defiance of the Indians' treaty rights.

Many of the other promises made by the whites were ignored. The meager cash payments were never awarded, and the money that did come from Washington to pay for Indian cattle and fodder was squandered by a few dishonest officials who pocketed the proceeds. Buildings the government had agreed to erect for the Indians' use were mere shells that lasted no more than one winter. Even the treaty tribes, as they were known to distinguish them from the Wal-lam-wat-kin band of "Lower" Nez Perce in the Wallowa Valley, were complaining.

The Indians were unaware that in the East whites were fighting one another in one of the bloodiest wars the world had ever known. Because most of the U.S. military were engaged in the Civil War, peace in the West had to be maintained through negotiations. The treaty of 1863 only added fuel to the conflict that was to come later.

In 1863 the Indians were asked to cede more than ten thousand square miles, including mines and rich agricultural land in Washington, Oregon, and Idaho. The lands to be ceded included the Wallowa Valley, the ancestral home of Tu-eka-kas's band in the state of Oregon. The Nez Perce always returned from their hunting trips to their permanent villages.

To the tribes who signed this treaty, it brought no loss, no change. They had not given up their ancestral lands; but for the non-treaty Nez Perce it meant they would be forced to abandon the Valley of Winding Waters—the sacred burial ground of their ancestors. Tu-eka-kas continued to ignore the rulings of the white Indian agents who changed from year to year, sometimes from month to month. It is said that when Tu-eka-kas learned that the Indian Bureau in Washington had decided that Lawyer's act of signing the treaty was binding upon all Nez Perce bands, he tore up his copy of the treaty and his copy of the New Testament, which he had kept since the day he was baptized by Missionary Spalding.

Young Joseph again accompanied his father to the council in 1863. He heard his father speak eloquently about the rights of those who had not agreed to give up their land. It was here young Joseph met one of his future wives, daughter of Chief Whisk-tasket of the treaty Nez Perce at Lapwai. In spite of the differences in their alliances with the whites, marriage was approved by both families, and elaborate ceremonies solemnized the nuptial.

Young Joseph was twenty-three years old. He was described as being six feet two inches tall, muscular, and adept at all physical sports. Yet he was a quiet, dignified young man even in his youth, respected by his elders and recognized as a leader.

As Tu-eka-kas began to grow blind and feeble, he depended on Young Joseph to assume his duties as chief of the Wal-lam-wat-kin band of the Wallowa Valley. It took a great deal of patience on Joseph's part to keep his people from reacting with violence. Settlers were moving into the valley. There were constant disputes over ownership of cattle and horses, but he was never able to get the whites to admit they were trespassing on land that was not theirs.

Among the non-treaty Nez Perce, a new faith was being preached by the prophet, Smohalla. He was not a Nez Perce but from a kindred tribe. He was afflicted with epilepsy, a disorder of the central nervous system characterized by convulsions and loss of consciousness. He capitalized on his misfortune by declaring that during these spells he spoke with spirits. He professed that his revelations came from dreams; thus those who followed the words were known as "Dreamers." He preached the gospel of passive resistance against the whites. He condemned his people for adopting agriculture and stock raising, basing his philosophy on the belief that the earth was their mother and that their present troubles came about because they had abandoned their own religion and violated the laws of nature.

He promised his people that an Indian would rise up to drive out their white enemies and would raise all Indians from the dead. He won many converts and even today there are some who practice the Dreamer religion.

The differences in religion between the non-treaty group, many of whom were Dreamers, and the treaty Indians, most of whom were Christians, added to the intertribal friction.

In the winter of 1871 Tu-eka-kas called Young Joseph to him and made him promise that he would never give up their homeland. The pledge was made. The old chief died holding his oldest son's hand.

Tu-eka-kas was dressed in his finest clothes. After two days of mourning, the body was tightly wrapped in deerskin and laid upon poles. Four warriors carried the bier to the waiting grave. The chief's head was placed facing east so that he might see the rising sun when entering the spirit world. Words were spoken describing his bravery. His two wives dressed in tattered clothing, cut their braids of hair, and threw the braids into the fire. The grave was covered with split cedar logs. On top of these, stones were piled to ward off any chance of desecration by prowling animals.

When the family of the dead chief returned to the village, their lodge was moved to a new location at once to prevent the ghost of the dead from causing harm to the living. A month later the family gave a great feast. All the friends of Tu-eka-kas were invited. Many of his personal possessions were given to the guests as a solemn remembrance of the days of his youth. Joseph was presented with his father's eagle-feather bonnet. It was a sign that the mantle of power and responsibility had been passed on to him.

Two years after Tu-eka-kas's death Joseph was asked to a council by the superintendent of Indian affairs for Oregon, T.B. Odeneal. It was held March 27, 1873 at Lapwai. It was the first council at which Joseph, then thirty-three years of age, represented his people. He did so with honesty and bravery.

Again he was told that all Nez Perce Indians were ordered to settle at once on the Lapwai Reservation. Joseph replied, "I did not want to come to this council, but I came hoping that we could save blood. The white man has no right to come here and take our country. We have not accepted any presents from the Government. Neither Lawyer nor any other chief had authority to sell this land. It has always belonged to my people. It came unclouded to them from our fathers, and we will defend this land as long as a drop of Indian blood warms the hearts of our men."

When Superintendent Odeneal insisted that they must leave the Valley of Winding Waters, Joseph's words left no doubt as to his intentions.

"I will not. I do not need your help; we have plenty, and we are contented and happy if the white man will let us alone. The reservation is too small for so many people with all their stock. You can keep your presents; we can go to your towns and pay for all we need; we have plenty of horses and cattle to sell, and we won't have any help from you; we are free now; we can go where we please. Our fathers were born here. Here they lived, here they died, here are their graves. We will never leave them."

Odeneal related the following conversation in his report to the secretary of the interior:

Joseph was asked, "Do you want schools or school houses on the Wallowa Reservation?"

The chief answered, "No."

When asked why, Joseph replied that then they would be forced to have churches. He did not want churches because, "They will teach us to quarrel about God, as the Catholics and Protestants do . . . We do not want to learn that. We may quarrel with men sometimes about things on this earth, but we never quarrel about God. We do not want to learn that."

Joseph asked that he might go to Washington to meet the great white leader, the president of the United States. His request was denied. It is interesting to wonder what changes might have come about if the two men, President Ulysses S. Grant and the peacemaker, as Chief Joseph was called, had met.

There were many whites who agreed with Joseph's logic, but Governor L.F. Grover of Oregon did not. He felt that the few hundred Indians living in the region of the Wallowa Valley would keep whites from making their homes there. The area he was trying to protect was the size of the state of Massachusetts, with overcrowding a less than serious argument. Even today there are few large towns. It is a semi-wilderness where sheepherders roam; yet this was the land that caused bloodshed and heartache for Indians and whites alike.

In 1874 the non-treaty Nez Perce held a meeting at the Weippe Prairie in Idaho near the start of the Lolo Trail to Montana. To make sure that there would be no violence, Agent Montieth and a company of cavalry attended the conference. It was learned that President Grant had issued a new proclamation on June 10, 1875 opening all of the Wallowa Valley to white settlement. The Valley of Winding Waters now became known as Union County.

The settlers who did take up land encouraged soldiers to drive the Indians out. They tried to accomplish this by sending in reports that Joseph's band of Indians was driving off and killing stock and threatening the lives of the settlers.

When the reports were investigated, it was found that Joseph and most of his band had been attending a feast celebration and had been no place near where the trouble was said to have taken place.

Another incident between two whites and an Indian, We-tot-yah, resulted in the death of an Indian over the theft of two horses. Again it was proved the Indian was blameless. The missing horses were found quietly grazing near the owner's ranch.

The family of the slain Indian demanded justice—the surrender of the guilty men. Troops were sent to stop any action of revenge. It was finally the daughter of the murdered We-tot-yah who stopped the war party saying she did not want other friends to be killed for the killing of one person. The matter was dropped but not forgotten.

Nor were the whites' orders forgotten. Joseph and his people were given a final warning. Acting under orders of the Indian Bureau, agent Monteith notified Joseph that he had until April 1, 1877 to come on to the reservation peacefully.

The most important white official in the area was General Oliver O. Howard, who had been appointed two years before to be the new commander of the Department of Columbia, with headquarters at Fort Vancouver. He and Joseph had met once. Joseph believed Howard to be a fair man. He wished to talk to him. Joseph sent word through his friend, Young Chief, head of the Umatillas, to Cornoyer, the Umatilla agent, asking for an interview with General Howard.

The following month Howard sent his aide-de-camp Lieutenant Boyle. Joseph said he would speak only to the general. Ollokot represented his brother at this meeting. He took along detailed maps of the Wallowa, Grande Ronde, and Imnaha valleys, to which the Wal-lam-wat-kins laid claim. Howard finally agreed to meet Joseph and other non-treaty chiefs at Lapwai later in the month. Runners were sent to notify Chiefs Looking Glass, White Bird, Hush-hush-kewt, and Tuhulhutsut.

The people led by Looking Glass lived on Clear Creek, a tributary of Clearwater River. This chief was the son of the old Chief Looking Glass who had signed the Treaty of 1855. The new Chief Looking Glass was some forty-five years old. The Nez Perce knew him as A-push-wa-hite. Among the whites he was known as a diplomat and a leader of peace.

White Bird, whose Nez Perce name was Pen-pen-hi-hi, meaning literally "White Pelican," was ready to fight the whites whenever he could gather warrior support. His people roamed among the steep mountains along the Salmon River that lay to the south of the reservation.

Hush-hush-kewt lived in the Asotin country of southeastern Washington on the south bank of the Snake River. He was not to be trusted, the whites felt.

Tuhulhutsut was one of the leading tewats of the Dreamer faith. Although his band along the Snake River was not large, he exerted great influence on those who were followers of Smohalla's religion. Like the prophet he was a great orator.

Joseph and Ollokot were by far the tallest of the chiefs. They were regarded with respect by Indians and whites alike, as was General Howard. Howard was courteous and thoughtful in his manner. He had earned his rank fighting valiantly in the War Between the States. He had lost an arm during the fighting and was known to the Indians as the "one-armed soldier-chief."

Howard informed the council that no matter how long the talks lasted they would still be ordered to move to the reservation. This did not seem to leave much room for compromise. White Bird hid his face behind a big eagle feather and kept silent, but when out of hearing of the white council members, he made threats that he planned to attack when the time was right.

Tuhulhutsut was the first to speak outright that he would never go on the reservation. General Howard then put the medicine man under arrest and had him placed in the guardhouse. This had a temporary restraining influence on the council, but it caused bitterness. The Indians now realized that all thought of compromise was past. They would have to comply with orders or fight. Joseph spoke for peace. It was decided that Joseph, Looking Glass, and White Bird would look at the land set aside for the Indians.

The inspection party was composed of the chiefs, General Howard, his aide Lieutenant Wilkinson, and an interpreter. They rode up the valley of Lapwai toward the mouth of Sweetwater Creek. Steep hills barren of trees flanked the valley. Two white families had marked off fields in the lowland and were already settled as farmers. General Howard promised that if this was land that any of the chiefs chose to maintain for hunting, the white settlers would be paid for their homesteads and not allowed on the reservation.

In the afternoon the party rode through extensive grazing pasture used by the white officials of the government Indian agency. The next day Agent Montieth and six cavalrymen joined the group. Also Joseph's brother Ollokot caught up with them to view the country. Everyone seemed to be in good spirits, except when the chiefs again approached General Howard to release the old tewat Tuhulhutsut from the guardhouse. They argued it was unfair that he was being held in prison simply for speaking his mind. General Howard was firm. The medicine man would be confined until the land matters were settled.

The next day, May 10, the party rode eighteen miles farther into the mountainous region. White Bird selected land in the vicinity of Kamia. Looking Glass chose to live farther down the Clearwater Valley. Joseph decided to go above Kamiah on the Clearwater, for he wished to be with friends whose lodges were in that direction.

The final meeting of all those concerned was held on May 15. Howard granted the Indians only thirty days to move onto the reserve. Joseph's band had the farthest to travel, but no concessions were made. When Joseph returned to his people, he found that soldiers were already occupying the Wallowa Valley. Again there was talk of refusing to move, but Joseph insisted that they leave immediately to avoid confrontation between his people and the policing soldiers.

Peace might have been preserved if it hadn't been for the three young braves of White Bird's band who went on a revenge-seeking attack against the white families along the Salmon River.

There were still some of the older warriors who counseled Joseph that there was no reason that there would be trouble. Joseph had not even been in camp when the killings occurred. But Joseph knew better. He and his people would be blamed. The soldiers would seek to punish them before the truth were known. It was then that Joseph committed his people to fight.

Timothy (above) and the Elder Joseph were the Reverend
Henry Spalding's first converts.
Yellow Bull (below left) was one of Chief Joseph's allies.
The treaty signed by Chief Lawyer (below right) in 1863 forced
the Nez Perce to abandon the Valley of Winding Waters—the
sacred burial ground of their ancestors.

Henry Spalding (above) had a Presbyterian mission where he spread the Christian faith and helped the Indians. He compiled a grammar of the Nez Perce language. His wife Elisa, shown at left with two young children, opened a school to teach the youngsters.

Left: General Oliver O. Howard was responsible for seeing that the Nez Perce moved to the reservation in Idaho. Chief Joseph surrendered to him.
Right: General John Gibbon's men attacked and killed about two hundred Nez Perce in the Battle of Big Hole.
Below: The army's pack train

Left: Josiah Red Wolf, the last survivor of the Nez Perce War
Below: A historic marker in Oregon shows where the Nez Perce Indian War started in 1877.

Left: Colonel Wood's thirteen-year-old son Erskine spent five months alone with Chief Joseph and his men.
Below: Chief Joseph, on the white horse behind the flag, attended the dedication of Ulysses S. Grant's tomb in 1897.

Above: A medallion commemorating Joseph, Chief of the Nez Perce   Below: Roasting beef on a framework of saplings to feed guests at Chief Joseph's funeral

An 1877 sketch of Fort Lapwai by an officer named
Cadachs on General Howard's staff

Chapter 5

INDIAN WARFARE

The news of the massacres spread. Many settlers in the area abandoned their homes and their livestock to seek safety at Fort Lapwai or in the town of Mount Idaho. Frantic wires were sent to the governor of Idaho Territory, Mason Brayman, urging him to send troops to wipe out the Indians, all Indians. Fear reached near hysteria.

The treaty Indians, wishing to keep their distance from the renegades, immediately started for the reservation. As they streamed past Fort Lapwai, they confirmed reports of a massacre. Even as they spoke more murders were taking place.

Some of White Bird's young warriors were on a rampage. Lew Day, who managed a trading post in Mount Idaho, volunteered to ride the sixty miles to Fort Lapwai to get help. He never reached his destination. Day was attacked by a raiding party but was able to escape and make his way to the Norton farm and stagecoach station. His wound was dressed. He mounted a fresh horse and then assisted a party of ten men, women, and children in a desperate attempt to return to Mount Idaho, only eighteen miles away.

They had not traveled far before they were attacked by

still another Indian war party. The horses hauling the wagon were quickly shot down, leaving the party stranded. John Chamberlain, his wife, and two children tried to escape into the brush. Chamberlain was killed in hand-to-hand fighting. His wife was severely wounded. The daughter's tongue was cut and the boy's head crushed.

The next day two more men of the settlers' group were killed. Norton was one of them. His wife was shot in both legs, but she, as well as Mrs. Chamberlain and her daughter, survived. They were saved because of the heroic efforts of Maude Bowers, who finally, by a roundabout route, reached Mount Idaho to give the alarm. A company of volunteers immediately left to bring in the wounded.

Joseph heard what was going on. He highly disapproved, but was powerless to stop it. Even White Bird, who had been in favor of war, tried to call his men back. He reasoned that killing settlers was only a waste of ammunition that should be used against the military.

Joseph spread out a few of his scouts on high points of land to keep track of army movements. Indian sentinels set fire to straw stacks on abandoned farms to reveal movements of the enemy. The coyote call from high ridges came from human throats to warn of the whites' approach.

General Howard had called up Troops F and H of the First Cavalry commanded by Captain David Perry. These men had not yet faced much of a challenge in Indian warfare. They were confident that as soon as they showed the strength of their firepower, the Indians would scatter.

Perry's force left Fort Lapwai on June fifteenth. They hoped to surprise the Indians at Cottonwood Creek; but, after a forced all-night ride, they found the Indians had already left that camp. The cavalry continued on to the town of Grangeville where they heard that Joseph's Nez Perce had been seen heading to White Bird Canyon. Perry surmised that they would likely be crossing the Salmon River at that point. If they successfully crossed the river there, they could go south to the Little Salmon, take the buffalo trail east and escape into Montana and then into Canada. Perry intended to stop them before this could happen.

Perry pushed his men farther, without sleep; he and his troops rode across the rolling prairie. They hoped to surprise the Indians under cover of darkness, but they were being watched. Again the single call of the coyote that ended unnaturally on a high note sounded the alarm.

To gain a more strategic defensive position, the Indians moved their camp to a small valley at the mouth of the stream where it flowed into the gorge. Behind them lay the Salmon River. The steep slopes of White Bird Canyon hid them from the whites' view.

In a lodge apart from the camp, Joseph's wife was about to have a baby. Joseph and his brother Ollokot stayed on guard to protect her. Ollokot borrowed a spyglass belonging to the

Indian herder, Old Blackfoot. They watched as Perry's men appeared over the crest of the first slope of the canyon. Joseph could stay with his family no longer.

Battle plans were quickly drawn up. Joseph ordered the women to take charge of the herd of horses and drive them downriver behind the bluffs. He then divided his fighting force into two main groups. Some were positioned on the high rocks where White Bird Canyon cut into the flat ground of the surrounding prairie. Another band of warriors was placed behind a ridge to the left of the camp. The braves and their war ponies reached their battle positions, where the well-trained animals stood silently beside their riders, ropes dragging on the ground, ready to respond to commands.

For four miles the route of the cavalry followed along a narrow canyon with a steep descent. The canyon walls were further cut at intervals by streams that flowed only during the season of melt. The western slope protruded like the backbone of some gigantic monster. To the east the land dipped into a series of grassy slopes.

Where the distance between the rock walls widened, the cavalry formed lines four abreast, guns ready. They were accompanied by civilian volunteers and by Indian scouts paid by the military.

There are differences of opinion as to who fired the first shot, but it was the Indians who soon assumed the offensive. While some of the warriors sniped at the soldiers from behind rocks, others mounted their ponies and pressed the attack.

One of the first shots from the Indians killed John Jones, Perry's trumpeter. It was an important loss. Only the sound of a bugle during the heat of battle could direct the cavalry. Shouted commands never carried over the noise of combat. The result was total confusion.

The two companies of cavalry became separated. Trimble's men, who had been serving as advance scouts, tried to work their way back along the canyon trail, while Perry's men broke for the top by the most direct route—straight up.

When Perry and the remnants of F Company reached the rim, they followed the ridge to the head of the trail. There were only twenty-two left of the original ninety-nine. The retreat now continued in a more orderly fashion, but Indians on ponies continued to harass the troops. Colonel Perry later wrote in a report that, "The Indians fought us to within four miles of Mount Idaho, and only gave it up on seeing that we would not be driven any further except at our own gait."

Another detachment of eighteen men under Lieutenant Theller had been acting as a rear guard, and sought escape up a narrow ravine that bisected the main canyon. Too late they discovered they had entered a dead end. Not one of them escaped death.

What was most humiliating for the soldiers about the defeat was that they outnumbered the Indians, yet only four Indians were known to have been wounded.

The Indians, in turn, had learned their lessons well from the military, flanking movements to cut the formation in two, making cavalry charges with a sudden change of direction. In contrast to the white soldier, the Indian was an excellent horseman taught from childhood. His pony was well-trained and obeyed its master without fail. Trimble noted that an Indian pony would stand and eat grass while its owner fought. A cavalry mount had to be held or it would soon bolt. The normal procedure was to detail every fourth man to hold his horse and the horses of three others. In other words, a company of cavalry that wanted to fight on foot had to reduce its fighting power by one quarter.

The Indians were cautious about not wasting ammunition. Contrary to popular belief, the Nez Perce rarely attempted to fire from horseback. It was too difficult to be accurate with old guns. The Nez Perce Indians always dismounted to fire unless their purpose was to stampede stock. When a warrior wanted to fire, he rolled off the pony to the ground, took deliberate aim, and crawled on again in a matter of seconds. The pony remained quiet and patient during the firing.

The Indians had gone into battle with only bows and arrows, old cap-and-ball revolvers, and a few antiquated rifles. Joseph's warriors were able to take guns from the dead soldiers to add to their limited arsenal. Now that they would be able to fight on more equal terms the results would be devastating.

There was great celebration in the Indian camp that night. There was dancing and feasting but Joseph's first thoughts were of his wife. During the heat of battle she had given birth to a baby daughter. Joseph gave the command that all were to remain in camp where they were. There was talk about pressing their advantage and directly attacking the fort. It is possible that this would have been a successful maneuver, but Joseph's main goal was to protect his people including women and children and elders.

In the meantime both forces had a chance to reorganize. The decisive victory brought a rush of young warriors from other tribes to Joseph's side. Colonel Perry, on the other hand, had to wait for more reserves to bolster the sadly depleted morale of the surviving troops.

Five days after Perry's battle, General Howard's column of infantry, cavalry, and artillery, under the command of Captain Marcus Miller, was on the march; but there was great disagreement within the settler population about where the troops should be sent. Howard declined to send them to Mount Idaho immediately because that would leave Lewiston and Lapwai unguarded. Volunteers resented the authority and slow tactics of the military.

Joseph called a war council with White Bird, Ollokot, Tuhulhutsut, and Yellow Bull to plan their own campaign. Joseph's scouts were well-informed of the military's movements. Joseph knew that another battle would have to be fought, but he wanted to be the one to choose the time and place. He waited until Howard's men had almost reached the Salmon River Valley. Then he moved his people down the river a few miles and crossed at Horseshoe Bend. Here they were placed in an excellent defensive position in the mountainous area.

The only way Howard could fight the Indians would be to meet them on a rocky wilderness battlefield. Joseph could then fall back and recross the river to the north, pass the troop's flank and cut off Howard's communications and supply from Fort Lapwai.

Crossing to the south bank of the river left Joseph three possible routes of escape if the superior number of white soldiers meant that a long siege was planned. He could turn south and hide in the Seven Devils country, an extremely rough and inaccessible mountain area, or farther south he could cut eastward on the buffalo trail, or he could recross the Snake River into Oregon and fight on his own land in Wallowa, every inch of which he knew by heart. It was a masterful plan.

On the twenty-fifth the general moved his troops to White Bird Canyon, the site of the devastating defeat of Perry's troops. Here the soldiers stopped to bury their dead. It was noted that no bodies had been scalped or mutilated as was the practice of most victorious Indian raiding parties.

Still there was no sign of the Nez Perce. Scouts were sent

along the crest of the canyon to report on any Indian activity. Campfires were seen rising from the rocky bluffs beside the Salmon. It was a trick to lure the soldiers in that direction. It worked. As the soldiers approached the river, Indian snipers rushed down from the ridge and taunted the soldiers to come after them. However when the command was given to open fire with long-range artillery, the Indians disappeared behind the rocks.

Finally several soldiers volunteered to swim the river and crawl to the top of the bluffs to direct the fire. To their amazement, when they reached the commanding position not an Indian was in sight. The Nez Perce snipers had accomplished their mission—to divert attention while Joseph and his main party were crossing to the north bank of the Salmon at Horseshoe Bend, fifteen or twenty miles away.

Unaware of this movement, Howard had made the decision to cross the Salmon with all his troops. The river was at flood stage. After considerable delay a log raft was built, thirty or forty feet long. A rope made from cavalrymen's lariats was stretched across the stream, but the swift current broke the line and sent the raft tumbling down the river. It was three days before the forces reached the other side.

During this time Howard had received word that some of Looking Glass's young warriors had joined the hostile Indians. To prevent more warriors from strengthening Joseph's command he ordered his troops to make a surprise attack on the camp of Looking Glass and to capture the chief and all his people.

Looking Glass was peacefully encamped on reservation land along Clear Creek. Although a few of his braves had joined Joseph's fighting force, no overt action had implicated him in the war.

On July first the troops attacked the camp. Looking Glass came forward under a flag of truce. Because his people were already on the reservation he could not see why they should be taken prisoner. He asked for time to talk to his people before making a surrender official. While negotiations were taking place, Washington Holmes, a volunteer, fired into the Indian camp. The Indians immediately fled eastward into the mountains, abandoning their lodges and over seven hundred ponies. It was an act that sent a peaceful tribe into war and gave Joseph another useful friend in Chief Looking Glass, who fought bravely during the entire campaign.

At Mount Idaho, Captain Stephen Whipple received word that Perry would arrive at Norton's ranch with an ammunition train. Joseph also was receiving accurate information about the army's movements. If he were to join forces with Looking Glass in the Clearwater Mountains he would have to cross the route taken by Perry. He also would have to prevent Whipple from attacking the men, women, and children in his command as they crossed the open Camas Prairie. Joseph led his people to the north of Cottonwood Ranch where Whip-

68

ple was waiting for reinforcements from Perry.

Each group waited for the other to make the first move. Whipple sent two citizen scouts to reconnoiter the territory where he expected the Indians to be camped close to water and to the south. One of the scouts returned with the news that they had been fired upon by Indians. This time Whipple sent Lieutenant Rains and ten volunteers to the aid of the missing scout, but when Rains entered a shallow ravine, the Indians sprang the trap and killed them all.

Whipple camped for the night but started in the morning of July fourth to meet Perry. Perry, unaware of the danger, was surprised to see Whipple's forces lined up as if for combat. He immediately rushed for the lines with his detail of twenty men and took charge.

Within two miles of the soldiers' position, some citizens on the Mount Idaho road were surrounded by Indians. There was an argument among the military whether they should go to the aid of the settlers and leave the ammunition unguarded, or stay where they were. At last a group of about twenty volunteers broke away, led by a Sergeant Simpson, who cried, "If your officers won't lead you, I will." Only after the civilians had stood off the Indian attack for a full hour did the military move ahead.

In the meantime the skirmish had occupied the troops just long enough for Joseph to lead the women and children and livestock they owned in a dash across the prairie to the wooded slopes of Horseshoe Mountain. Joseph had proved that an Indian, unschooled in the tactics of West Point military strategy, could succeed in outwitting the white soldiers for nearly a month.

Chapter 6

ON THE MOVE

Joseph hurried to join forces with Looking Glass, who was camped a few miles from Grangeville at the mouth of Cottonwood Creek as it entered the South Fork of the Clearwater River. Here there was excellent forage for their ponies, good fishing in the streams, and plenty of large game in the mountains to the east. They had hoped to spend time here giving families and animals a few days of relief. In the meantime General Howard's scouts had tracked the Indians' whereabouts, and the army was about to start in pursuit.

It took more than two days for the military to haul their heavy artillery guns up steep muddy trails. Rain added to their misery. The soldiers were without bedding or food until their supply train caught up with them. In spite of the hardships, Howard pressed his forces on in another attempt to surprise Joseph's forces.

On the morning of July 11, Howard's command had reached a high ridge above the river. They set up a howitzer and two gatling guns. They could see the Indian ponies grazing below them, guarded by herders. Shells were lobbed over the heads of the livestock in the hopes of causing a stampede. Alerted by the explosions, warriors dashed out to support the herders.

Others mounted war ponies and galloped ahead to strike the left flank of the soldiers' advancing line. Still another sortie of warriors opened fire on the right. The soldiers held their position until reinforcements arrived, but there were many casualties.

Undaunted by the fire of the gatling guns, the Indians charged to within a few feet of the soldiers' barricades. Joseph was everywhere along the line, shouting commands and directing flanking movements. It was easy to spot the chief. Unlike his men, he did not strip off his clothes for battle, as was the Indian custom. He wore his shirt, breechcloth, and moccasins. Apparently Joseph was determined to live down the reputation of coward some had given him when he had tried to negotiate peace with the whites.

The Indians spread out over hillsides and ravines, appearing just long enough to take aim and fire, and then disappearing into the wooded and rocky landscape. Much of the white firepower was wasted. With darkness, both sides cut off the attack. The Indians held possession of the battlefield's water supply. Horses and soldiers suffered. When daylight came the fighting resumed.

In the distance to the south, a dust cloud announced the arrival of the military supply train. It was escorted by a troop of cavalry commanded by Captain Jackson. A group of Indians on fast ponies raced to cut off the train before it reached the troops. Howard countered with a full charge to stop the

Indians. It was a desperate race, the outcome determining who could win the battle. The Indian attackers were far outnumbered. When there was nothing more they could do, they fled over almost impossible terrain, rocks and precipices so steep few horsemen dared to follow.

The ranks of the Nez Perce were now broken. They left behind food and clothing and valuable hides used for their lodges in their haste to reach safety. But Joseph reorganized his people and retreated in good order toward Kamiah. Actually their losses in fighting men had been few. Neither side had won a decisive victory. Howard boasted that the Indians had been driven from the Idaho Territory. For Joseph and his people the long journey had just begun.

On July 13 Joseph and his forces crossed the Clearwater River a mile above the Kamiah Ferry. Howard's cavalry were right behind them on the opposite bluff. Joseph's warriors opened fire that threw the cavalry into a state of confusion.

Howard's official report was that, "... our men jumped from their horses, and ran to the cover of the fences. Little damage resulted, except the shame to us, and a fierce delight to the foe."

Joseph was surprised that the army had been so swift in pursuit. He realized that the survival of his people depended on their reaching the Lolo Trail in the Bitterroot Mountains before being cut off by the soldiers. If his people were to continue east, they would be distancing themselves from the homeland for which they were fighting. One more time Joseph asked for a meeting with Howard to see if a peaceful solution could still be reached. Many felt this was just a ploy to delay action so the Indians could better prepare for their escape.

Whatever Joseph's intentions may have been, no truce was negotiated. Howard demanded that the Indians surrender their arms, ammunition, and horses. Joseph would be tried by a military court. Now it was clear to the Nez Perce that they would have to outrun the troops.

To prevent the Indians from reaching the head of the escape route, Howard dispatched a battalion of cavalry to cut them off before they reached their goal. However Joseph's scouts were now well aware of every move made by the military. They planned their own ambush.

The Indians carefully sawed partway through a number of trees bordering the trail. They buried the sawdust under leaves and replaced bark over the saw marks. A party of fifty or sixty warriors hid in the underbrush ready to charge and push the trees across the pass when the soldiers approached. Everything was ready.

Joseph's men watched as the advance scouting party of five Indians hired by Howard's fighting force passed by. No attack was to be made until the main military force entered the scene of ambush. The maneuver would have succeeded if the troops had not heard a shot and stopped to reconnoiter. One of the horses nervously pawing the ground, unearthed the sawdust. The officers dismounted and quickly discovered the cleverly hidden saw marks. The troops made a hasty retreat before the Indians could block their trail.

The Indians were on the move again. General Howard felt that his job was accomplished. There would be no more murders or burning of property. He was ready to recall his troops to their home base, but this was not to be the end of the campaign. Howard received further orders from army headquarters in Washington, D.C., that he was to pursue and capture the rebelling tribes of the Nez Perce nation.

To do the job efficiently General Howard needed more support. After wiring for reinforcements, he had to wait eight days for Major Green and his troops to arrive from Fort Boise. In the meantime Joseph's people were pushing ahead over the steepest of trails, which was frequently blocked by rock slides and fallen timber. Rain had made the trail slippery and dangerous. Many animals were abandoned along the way. The descending trail on the east side was even more dangerous. At times only a narrow ledge hung out over a deep canyon. Horses and ponies had to be led over the most hazardous sections. Some fell to their death below.

Only when the trail wound through a green valley dotted with hot sulfur springs, did Joseph give the order to stop and rest. The sick and wounded were treated with the "medicine" waters. The animals rested while hunting parties brought in game for the cooking pots.

Joseph had hoped that they would be welcomed by Chief Charlot's band of Flathead Indians, but his former ally refused to help for fear his own people would be attacked by the soldiers. Other tribes like the Crow had promised them a safe passage to the buffalo hunting grounds; however, this meant a detour to the south away from Canada and the land they hoped would give them temporary freedom.

Word of their coming preceded them. The citizens of Missoula, Montana, were now on the alert. All had visions of being massacred by the invading Nez Perce who had managed to outfight and outwit the soldiers to the west.

Volunteers were called up. Log fortifications were hastily thrown up across the canyon trail to block the path of the Indians. The fort to the south of the town was still under construction. The post was guarded by no more than forty-four soldiers. It was estimated that Joseph's band had more than 300 warriors and 450 women and children, many of whom could handle a gun as well as any man.

By July 26 the main body of Indians was within sight of the barricade. They made camp some two miles away and settled down to study what route they would take next. A direct attack would be foolhardy because of their position, even though they outnumbered their opponents.

Again, this time with Chief Looking Glass heading a peace mission, they tried to negotiate a truce. Captain Rawn, who was in charge, was not in a position to make a deal.

In the meantime the Indians again organized to move on. On the morning of July 29 the Indian cavalcade began climbing the canyon walls a half mile in front of the left side of the barricade. Gullies and trees on the south side of the gorge screened their movements from the soldiers.

An eyewitness among the ranks of the military later wrote, "About ten o'clock we heard singing, apparently above our heads. Upon looking up we discovered the Indians passing along the side of the cliff, where we thought a goat could not pass, much less an entire tribe of Indians with all their impedimenta."

Again the Nez Perce had slipped out of a trap. Joseph's current challenge was to keep his people together. Looking Glass and Joseph were in favor of heading for the country of the friendly Crow Indians. Pile of Clouds wanted to return to the Salmon River. White Bird remained neutral. Agreement was reached that they would remain as one group at least for the time being. They also agreed that there would be no bloodshed or criminal actions while they were among the people of Montana unless they were attacked.

They traded for supplies in the town of Stevensville, thirty miles up the Bitterroot River from Missoula by paying for goods with currency, gold dust coins, and greenbacks, acting as law-abiding citizens.

"We understood that there was to be no war," Joseph said later. "We intended to go peacefully to buffalo country, and leave the question of returning to our country to be settled afterwards."

There were battles ahead still to be fought.

Chapter 7

"I WILL FIGHT NO MORE FOREVER"

Joseph's people headed for the Big Hole Valley in Montana. It was a beautiful prairie basin of rolling hills and meadow encircled by green forested mountains. They erected their hide-covered tipis on the banks of Ruby Creek where it joined Trail Creek.

Looking Glass and Joseph agreed that this was a fine place for their people to rest and replenish their food supplies, but White Bird urged that they travel farther, putting as much distance as possible between themselves and General Howard's troops. One of the medicine men predicted that death was on their trail. It was not hard to imagine the truth to the forecast, yet it was too pleasant a spot to leave willingly.

They had no way of knowing that Howard had already sent messages by wire to Colonel John Gibbon at Fort Shaw just east of the Rocky Mountains. Gibbon's troops made the 150-mile march through difficult terrain to Missoula, Montana, in just seven days. Here they joined Rawn's command; this brought the total force to some 190 men.

Scouts were sent out to determine where the Nez Perce were. It was an easy trail to follow, sometimes a 150-foot-wide path trampled by hundreds of ponies and furrowed by dragging travois poles. Gibbon set up his own camp only a few hours' march behind the Indians and sent Lieutenants Bradley and Jacobs to reconnoiter the countryside.

When the advance soldiers glimpsed the Indian village from a high promontory, they saw an idyllic scene of family life. Hundreds of Indian ponies grazed in the meadow below them. Some women were cutting lodge poles for their tipis. Others were cooking. Children played close by.

It surprised the soldiers that they had not been detected. Usually Joseph had been very careful to post sentinels at least a mile or two from camp, guarding every direction of possible attack. The scouts left silently to bring their message back to headquarters. When Gibbon heard the news, he prepared his men for a night march and a surprise attack. They had to cross a swampy area and then a stream before opening fire, but they were able to approach without being seen. In the early gray of dawn an Indian on horseback headed toward the pony herd. The soldiers were so well concealed in the tall grass that he almost ran into them. Quickly shots were fired, and both Indian and mount went down.

Before the village could rouse itself, the infantry surged ahead, firing one round after another. In an instant the peaceful village became a scene of confusion. Women and children rushed for the cover of a willow bank close by. Others snatched babies in their arms and waded into the stream to hide along the marshy bank.

Warriors grabbed their guns and began returning fire. As the soldiers overran the village, it was a battle of hand-to-hand combat. Rifles were often used as clubs. Tomahawks and hunting knives helped stop the line of infantry that kept pushing forward. Indian women took up the attack using whatever weapons were at hand.

Within twenty minutes the village had been taken, the tipis set afire. Chiefs Joseph, White Bird, and Looking Glass tried to rally their forces along the riverbank. The soldiers were caught in a withering cross fire from sharpshooters in the hills and those hidden in thickets near the river.

Gibbon formed his men in a double line and charged the Indians through the brush, only to have the Nez Perce retreat more deeply into the stand of willows. To save his troops from further injuries, Gibbon gave the order to move back up a hill. This gave the soldiers time to tend to their wounded; but it also gave the Indians time to round up some of their horses and to search for their families.

The scene of carnage was a grisly one. Two of Joseph's four wives were dead, although the mother of his newborn daughter was safe with their child. The oldest daughter of Chief Looking Glass was shot through the head. The wounded were scattered from the creek to the wooded edge of the battlefield. In many cases it was the women who had braved cross fire in search of their wounded husbands and brothers, hiding them until they were strong enough to be moved.

To give his warriors cover to return to the smoldering ruins of the lodges, Joseph set fires in the grass to the north. With the wind blowing toward the hill, he hoped to smoke out Gibbon's troops and attack them when they ran from the flames that were fast crawling up the hillside. A change in the direction of the wind averted a catastrophe for the soldiers, but a dense smoke screen gave Joseph a chance to collect his people and what possessions they had left.

In spite of the fact that Joseph had been in the thick of battle and had his horse shot from under him, he had escaped serious wounds. He again had proved his leadership, bravery, and power, but the price had been a bitter one. Joseph later estimated that 220 of his people had been killed in what was later called the Battle of Big Hole; yet, he had managed to rally his warriors to retake the village, to bury the dead, and to salvage supplies.

General Howard wrote, "Few military commanders, with good troops, could better have recovered after so fearful a surprise."

Now the Nez Perce headed south and east, but this time they were not to be surprised. A rear guard was always on the alert. White Cloud attempted to get help from the Shoshone Indians, who had in the past been their enemies. When this failed, Joseph realized that they would have to depend on their own resources and the speed with which they could travel.

General Howard planned to cut off the Indians before they could reach Yellowstone; however the Nez Perce crossed the stage road ahead of the troops. They camped on the Camas Meadows about a day's march ahead of the troops.

Joseph proposed a plan to scatter or capture the horses of the cavalry. Indians always traveled with spare mounts, but when on maneuvers, the soldiers were limited to the animals they were riding. Without horses, they would be helpless.

Under cover of darkness, a group of Joseph's men cut the ropes of 150 mules that carried supplies and hauled wagons. Firing into their midst and waving buffalo blankets, they stampeded the animals away from camp. The Indians had hoped to do the same with the cavalry mounts, but the first sound of attack had brought the soldiers to battle stations.

The camp was thrown into wild confusion—a reversal of positions from the Battle of Big Hole. As they mounted their horses in pursuit of the Indians and the mules, they were attacked on two sides by waiting Nez Perce hidden for an ambush. The troops promptly retreated until they could organize a spearhead attack. Joseph did not press his advantage further. He was biding time to give his people a chance to put distance between them and their pursuers.

During the early weeks of their exodus Joseph had been able to keep his warriors under control, forbidding them to take vengeance on civilians. Since the devastating losses at the Battle of Big Hole, some young warriors delighted in taking their revenge. Two parties of tourists within Yellowstone Park were captured by renegade bands of Indians. One man was killed and several were wounded while attempting to escape. The tourists were taunted with threats of torture. When Joseph heard of the actions he was angry, but all he could do in amends was to protect the prisoners and send them on their way when they were close to troops who could take over their care.

Colonel Samuel D. Sturgis's Seventh Cavalry now was ordered to overtake the Nez Perce. Howard's command was not far behind, but Joseph prevented communication between the two forces by killing every courier sent to relay messages. It was Sturgis's job to guard the various passes through the eastern slope of the mountains, a distance of some 250 miles. His scouts gave him the information that the country was too rough and broken for the Indians to cross over to Clarks Fork. It was supposed the Indians would follow the usual route to the Stinking Water River.

Joseph feigned flight along this trail, but then abruptly turned his forces north. They gained a heavily timbered ridge, passed through a narrow canyon that opened abruptly into the Clarks Fork Valley, and slipped by the guard posts Sturgis had set up. To further confuse his enemy, Joseph sent a few of his young men on the other side of Sturgis' force toward Hart Mountain. At daybreak, they stirred up a great dust cloud by tying sagebrush to their lariats and dragging the bundles of brush along the ground.

Sturgis was completely fooled into believing that he was chasing the main band of Nez Perce, while in reality the main body of Indians marched through the pass to the north. When Sturgis discovered the deception, he ordered his men to press on at top speed. He hoped that Joseph would relax his guard, thinking they were way ahead of their pursuers.

About seven miles from Canyon Creek the soldiers overtook the Indians in a narrow wash with banks from ten to twenty feet high. The soldiers charged in. The Indians fought hard and retreated slowly to give the women, children, and older men a chance to escape through the canyon. They kept on the move all night, and the next day had to fight a large party of River Crow Indians, who had reinforced Sturgis' men.

Joseph now led his people west of the Judith Mountains, and on September 23 crossed the Missouri River at Cow Island where a freight depot was located. The Indians took what supplies they needed and burned the rest.

The country from the valley of Clarks Fork to the Bearpaw Mountains is a rolling plateau. Unaware that there was another army in the field chasing them, the Nez Perce moved on at a leisurely pace. Joseph believed that his people were safe.

They reached the northern slope of the Bearpaw Mountains, which was within an easy day's march of the Canadian border. Joseph sent runners to find Chief Sitting Bull of the

Sioux, who had already crossed into Canada; he proposed that the two bands of Indians join forces if either of them were attacked. An agreement was never reached.

In the meantime another army had joined the attack. Colonel Miles, with 375 men, had reached the Missouri at the mouth of Musselshell Creek on September 23. Miles commandeered a river steamer and ferried his troops across the Missouri. He was careful to follow a trail that kept a range of the Little Rockies between his soldiers and the position the Indians held. To keep his movements secret as long as possible, he ordered the soldiers not to hunt or disturb the wildlife that they frequently encountered.

The Indians were surprised to learn that still more reinforcements were aligned against them, but they had learned lessons of defense from the soldiers. They had dug trenches and were prepared to fight when the cavalry mounted a charge. They carefully held their fire until the soldiers were within one hundred feet of their rifle pits. They chose their targets well. Whenever they heard a voice raised in command, they directed their fire there. Without officer commanders, there was confusion in the ranks, but both sides fought bravely and ferociously.

When the first attack began, Joseph was on the opposite side of the creek from the Indian camp with his twelve-year-old daughter. "I gave her a rope, and told her to catch a horse and join the others who were cut off from the camp," he said later, remembering the fateful day when he saw her for the last time.

Then he fought his way back to the center of the battle. The first wave of soldiers were forced to retreat, but Joseph lost many of his own chiefs. His own brother Ollokot fell, and so did Tuhulhutsut, Looking Glass, and Pile of Clouds. In spite of personal tragedy, Joseph kept up the fight.

When the troops resumed their attack on the second day, the Indians had dug even deeper trenches, some connected by underground passages. The women used whatever was at hand, knives or frying pans, to dig shelter.

After receiving considerable losses themselves, Miles and his men withdrew for the second time and prepared to lay siege to the camp. He was worried that Sitting Bull might still come to the rescue of the Nez Perce and stage another Custer massacre.

The weather worsened. Snow whipped into a blizzard on the night of September 30. Miles sent for reinforcements. Sturgis and Howard were on their way.

On the morning of October 1, Miles started negotiations for the Indians to surrender. Joseph sent Yellow Bull, a subchief, as his representative, but later decided to meet with the soldiers himself. General Miles held Joseph in camp overnight as a hostage. In return, the Indians captured Lieutenant Jerome of the Second Cavalry; he had been sent to spy on the Indian encampment and report their strength.

Finally an agreement was made to exchange prisoners, so that Joseph could go back and consult with the surviving chiefs under his control. They could have escaped from Bear Paw Mountain if they had been willing to leave the wounded and women and children behind, but this was not to be. Again the fighting resumed.

General Howard's troops joined Miles' command on October 4. Now there was no hope for the Indians' cause. Sitting Bull had refused to help. Two Nez Perce scouts of the treaty tribes were sent to Joseph's camp to offer the terms of surrender.

As Joseph understood the terms, General Miles promised that the Indians, after laying down their arms, would be returned to the Lapwai reservation.

At 2:30 P.M. on October 5, 1877 all firing ceased. Around 4 P.M. Joseph rode from his camp. His rifle lay across his knees. His head was bowed. His scalp lock was tied with otter fur. The rest of his hair hung in thick braids on either side of his face. He wore buckskin leggings and a gray woolen shawl. It was noted that his clothing was pierced by more than a dozen bullet holes.

He swung off his horse and offered his rifle to General Howard. Instead the general motioned that the surrender would be to his subordinate Colonel Miles who had fought so bravely. The weapon was laid on the ground. Then Chief Joseph stepped back to give his formal speech of surrender. His last words were, "Hear me, my chiefs, I am tired; my heart is sick and sad. From where the sun now stands, I will fight no more forever."

From then on a straggling band of prisoners filed into Miles's camp on Eagle Creek. It was later learned that White Bird and a band of 104 Nez Perce had escaped the picket's lines and had joined Sitting Bull in Canada. Joseph's twelve-year-old daughter was among them. His infant daughter and young wife were with Joseph at the surrender.

Above: A photo of Chief Joseph taken about 1898
Below: The Chief Joseph Monument at Nespelem,
Washington, was dedicated in 1905.

Chapter 8

BROKEN PROMISES

Joseph was assured by both General Howard and General Miles that his people would soon be sent to the Lapwai Reservation. While this was not their beloved Valley of the Winding Waters, it would be familiar surroundings, with mountains, running streams, and plentiful game. But first they were to be taken to Fort Keogh, which lay on the south bank of the Yellowstone River near the mouth of the Tongue River and the present site of Miles City.

The Nez Perce were given a comfortable camp. In later reports, Miles agreed that he intended to keep them there during the winter and send them back to Oregon in the spring. Within ten days orders were changed. Someone in Washington had decided that they would be sent eight hundred miles by steamer to Fort Lincoln near Bismarck, North Dakota. It was reasoned that it would be cheaper to keep them there.

General of the army, W.T. Sheridan, proclaimed that the Nez Perce should never be allowed to return to Oregon or to Lapwai. It was thought that the settlers in that region would never accept the Nez Perce Indians for fear they would try to reclaim their land. Yet it had been White Bird's band, not Joseph's, that had started the war, and it was Joseph who had shown all along that his word was always kept.

Since the river level was low on the Yellowstone, fourteen flatboats were commandeered to transport the Nez Perce from Fort Keogh. Each boat could accommodate between twenty and twenty-five people. The wounded, the sick, and the elderly and children were put aboard. One white took charge of each boat to handle the tiller and to guard the prisoners. It's interesting to note the trust the guards placed in the peaceful intent of these Indians. They lent guns to Indian hunters to help provide rations along the way.

Chief Joseph and all able-bodied warriors and their families marched overland to Fort Lincoln. Here they were greeted by the press and curious onlookers and were treated to dinner at the luxurious Sheridan House in Bismarck. A fine meal was no substitute for broken promises.

From Fort Lincoln, the Nez Perce were sent to Fort Leavenworth in Kansas. Used to a mountain plateau country where the mountain streams were cold and clear, they could not stand the hot, swampy lowlands of the Missouri River bottomland. Malaria was rampant, and the only water they had for cooking or drinking was river water already contaminated by white settlers. Many of Joseph's people sickened and died.

Both Miles and Howard tried in vain to influence Washington to send the Nez Perce back to Oregon. Instead, the next move was to territory on both sides of the Salt Fork River of Arkansas. Shortly afterwards, about one-fourth of the survivors died, largely due to the malaria they had contracted at Leavenworth.

Joseph continued to seek protection for his people. During the summer of 1878 he received permission to go to Washington to plead his own case before the Great Chief, President Rutherford B. Hayes. Joseph knew that he could never turn back the time to when his people were entirely free, but he asked that they be treated as any other human being.

In an interview with President Hayes he said, "I know that my race must change. We cannot hold our own with white men as we are. We only ask an even chance to live as other men live. We ask to be recognized as men. We ask that the same law shall work alike on all men. If the Indian breaks the law, punish him by the law. If the white man breaks the law, punish him also.

"Let me be a free man—free to travel, free to stop, free to work, free to trade where I choose, free to choose my own teachers, free to follow the religion of my fathers, free to think and talk and act for myself—and I will obey every law, or submit to the penalty."

The result of these eloquent words was that the Nez Perce were removed to the Ponca Reservation in June of 1879. Their health did not improve. This period of mourning was harder on Joseph's people than the battles they had so bravely fought.

Six years later in the spring of 1885, a compromise was reached. Two hundred sixty-eight Nez Perce were divided into two parties; one group went, under military escort, to the Lapwai Reservation. The remaining 150, Joseph among them, were to proceed to the Colville Reservation at Nespelem, Washington.

The Indians were in a destitute condition, short of food, clothes patched and worn out, yet Joseph kept his dignity and his presence of command. He had gained a certain notoriety as a heroic and tragic figure even among the whites.

In 1889 he was asked to come to Portland, Oregon, to sit for a bas-relief portrait by sculptor Olin Warner. While there he met Colonel C.E.S. Wood, who had been one of Howard's officers during the Nez Perce campaign. Joseph invited Wood's thirteen-year-old son, Erskine, to visit him on the reservation. No greater confidence in Joseph's integrity could have been shown than when the colonel entrusted his son to the care of his former enemy.

In 1892 Erskine spent five months alone with Joseph and his band. He went on hunts with the tribe and was present at dances and feasts. With Chief Joseph's teaching, Erskine learned the Indians' customs and arts. He described the Indian camp as being two or more long rows of tipis and lodges. Sometimes three or more families would occupy the larger lodges. Several fires might be burning at the same time, the better to dry their meat for the winter season.

It was twelve more years before Joseph went east and then as a celebrity. He rode beside Buffalo Bill in the dedication of

Grant's tomb, but he was restless to get "home" where he could see grass and trees.

He never gave up his dream that some day his people could return to their ancestral land. Once more, in 1903, he went to Washington to petition President Theodore Roosevelt to grant his tribe the Wallowa Valley. By this time too many settlers had moved there. Again his request was denied. He accepted invitations to talk to groups of whites to plead his cause. On one of these trips he spoke before an audience at the University of Washington. The next day he attended a football game, which he watched in amazement.

Toward the end of his life, he would sit beside his campfire, speaking to no one, perhaps dreaming of the different life he had once led. On September 21, 1904 he was sitting before his fire as usual. Without warning he fell forward, dead. The agency physician said that Joseph had died of a broken heart.

He was quietly buried on reservation property, but the following year a white marble shaft seven-and-a-half feet in height was erected in his memory. On one side of the column a fine likeness of the warrior chief is carved, and below it appears his name in raised letters, "Chief Joseph." On another side is his Indian name "Hin-Mah-Too-Yah-Lat-kekt," and the English translation, "Thunder-Rolling-in-the-Mountains." On a third side is written, "He led his people in the Nez Perce War of 1877. Died 21 September, 1904, age, about 60 years."

Indians and whites together celebrated the dedication.

There was a formal distribution of Joseph's property. The great war bonnets and clothing went to three nephews. Only fourteen of Chief Joseph's horses were given away. The others were left for his two surviving widows, an investment that would keep them provided for the rest of their lives.

Everyone received some kind of gift, but the gift that he left the world was a lesson in tolerance, bravery, and honesty.

CHIEF JOSEPH 1840–1904

1840 Chief Joseph is born in the Wallowa Valley of the Winding Waters in Oregon. Construction begins on the Houses of Parliament in London, England.

1841 President William Henry Harrison, ninth president of the U.S., dies one month after his inauguration; Zachary Taylor becomes president. Great Britain's sovereignty is proclaimed over Hong Kong. Scottish surgeon James Braid discovers hypnosis. The first university degrees are granted to women in America.

1842 Gold is discovered in California. Nez Perce bands hold a meeting at Lapwai with white people. Seminole Indian War ends (started 1833) in Florida. The Webster-Ashburton Treaty defines the border between Canada and the U.S. The Treaty of Nanking ends the Opium War between Great Britain and China.

1843 John C. Fremont crosses the Rocky Mountains to California. Congress grants Samuel F.B. Morse $30,000 to build the first telegraph line from Washington, D.C. to Baltimore, Maryland.

1844 James Knox Polk is elected eleventh president of the U.S. Wood pulp paper is invented.

1845 Ollokut, brother of Chief Joseph, is born. Young Joseph is baptized. The Maori of New Zealand stage an uprising against British rule. Joshua Heilman patents a machine for combing cotton and wool. The U.S. Naval Academy is opened at Annapolis, Maryland.

1846 Quarrel develops between Old Joseph (Chief Joseph's father), a converted Christian, and the white missionaries at Lapwai. The Oregon Country is formally added to the U.S. when international borders are settled by a treaty between the United States and Great Britain. U.S. forces occupy New Mexico territory. Brigham Young leads the Mormons to the Great Salt Lake in Utah. John Deere constructs a steel plow.

1847 Charlotte Brontë publishes *Jane Eyre*. Emily Brontë publishes *Wuthering Heights*. Gold discoveries in California lead to the first U.S. gold rush.

1848 A meeting is held between General Palmer and Chief Joseph and his Nez Perce tribe. Oregon Territory is established. U.S. government acquires territories inhabited by some 150,000 Indians in California, Nevada, Utah, Arizona, New Mexico, Texas, and part of Colorado by several treaties. Switzerland becomes a federal union. The first British settlers arrive in New Zealand.

1849 Zachary Taylor is inaugurated as president of the U.S. *Who's Who* begins publication. Amelia Bloomer begins American women's dress reform.

1850 Henry Clay's compromise slavery resolutions are laid before the U.S. Senate. George Stephenson's cast-iron railroad bridge is opened at Newcastle, England.

1851 The first double-decker bus is introduced. Gold is found in Victoria, New South Wales, Australia. *The New York Times* begins publication.

1852 Franklin Pierce is elected president of the United States. The Niagara Falls suspension bridge is built.

1853 Vincent van Gogh is born. The first railroad is built through the Alps, from Vienna to Trieste.

1854 By a treaty with the U.S. government, the Omaha Indians give up their land and move to the Omaha Reservation some 70 miles north of the Missouri River. Kansas and Nebraska become U.S. territories. The Kansas-Nebraska Act limits area of the Indian Territory in present-day Oklahoma. Omaha is formally founded in the Nebraska Territory. Republican party is formed at Ripon, Wisconsin.

99

1855 The first U.S. institution to grant academic degrees to women, the Elmira Female College, is founded at Elmira, New York. A campaign against the Sioux Indians is led by Colonel W.S. Harney. Henry Wadsworth Longfellow writes *The Song of Hiawatha*. Livingston discovers Victoria Falls in Africa. Ferdinand de Lesseps is granted concession by France to build the Suez Canal. Old Joseph attends the Walla Council. U.S. government agents start making treaties with the bands of the Nez Perce Indians, exchanging Indian lands for the guaranteed reservation tracts, homes, schools and other facilities — as the result of these treaties the Native American lands are cut to a fraction of their original size. A council is held at the Walla council grounds between whites and five thousand members of the Nez Perce tribes; Chief Lawyer, claiming to be the majority head of Nez Perce tribes, signs the treaty; from now on his supporters are known as Treaty Nez Perce.

1856 The Rogue River War forces most of the Indians in northern California and southern Oregon to accept living on reservations. Indian massacre of Potawatomie Creek, Kansas, takes place. The first railway bridge to span the Mississippi River is opened between Davenport, Iowa, and Rock Island, Illinois. The first Australian cricket match is held.

1857 James Buchanan is inaugurated as the fifteenth president of the U.S. The Sepoy Mutiny against British rule in India is crushed. Elisha G. Otis installs the first safety elevator.

1858 Minnesota becomes a U.S. state. An "Expedition Against Northern Indians" is carried out by U.S. army troops to discourage attacks on Washington settlements. First Atlantic cable is completed by Cyrus W. Field, but it fails to operate. The Lincoln-Douglas debates are held in Illinois. The Suez Canal Company is formed. The National Association of Baseball Players is organized in America.

1859 Oregon becomes a U.S. state. First commercially productive oil well is drilled near Titusville, Pennsylvania. *On the Origin of Species* by Charles Darwin is published. The steamroller is invented. Work on the Suez Canal is begun under the direction of Ferdinand de Lesseps.

1860 Abraham Lincoln is elected president. The first pony-express line is started between Sacramento, California, and St. Joseph, Missouri. The first horse-drawn tram begins operation. Skiing becomes a competitive sport. Gold is discovered on the Nez Perce Reservation.

1861 Kansas becomes a U.S. state. Lewiston is incorporated as a gold-mining town in Nez Perce County, Idaho. American Civil War begins (ends 1865). Seven southern states set up the Confederate States of America with Jefferson Davis as president. Confederate forces repel Union forces at the first Battle of Bull Run. First transcontinental telegraph line is put in operation.

1862 The Santee Sioux in Minnesota rebel against mistreatment by white people on their reservation and kill about 800 settlers; as punishment, their land is confiscated and the Sioux are moved to Dakota Territory. Land Grant Act is approved, eventually leading to the establishment of the state university system. Swiss humanist Jean-Henri Dunant proposes the foundation of an international relief organization — the Red Cross. Many Civil War veterans settle in the western states under free land terms of the 1862 Homestead Act. In direct violation of the previous treaties, some fifteen thousand white settlers, mostly gold miners, are settled on Nez Perce Reservation. Fort Lapwai is built in Idaho for the protection of the whites and to prevent clashes between whites and the Indians (Fort Lapwai is now the headquarters of the Nez Perce Indian Agency).

1863 West Virginia becomes a U.S. state. Arizona and Idaho are organized as territories. Battle of Gettysburg. Whitestone Indian battle in North Dakota. Colonel Kit Carson is ordered to subdue the Navajo Indians in New Mexico. Lapwai Council is called and the Nez Perce reservation land is reduced from 10,000 square miles to 1,000 square miles. Lincoln issues the Emancipation Proclamation, freeing "all slaves in areas still in rebellion." Congress establishes free mail delivery. Roller skating is introduced to America.

1864 Nevada becomes a U.S. state. During the Sand Creek massacre of Cheyenne and Arapaho Indians in Colorado, some 900 U.S. cavalrymen kill 150-500 Indian men, women, and children. General William Tecumseh Sherman marches through Georgia. Abraham Lincoln is reelected president. "In God We Trust" first appears on U.S. coins.

1865 General Robert E. Lee surrenders at Appomattox Court House, Virginia. The American Civil War ends (started 1861). President Lincoln is assassinated; he is succeeded by Andrew Johnson. The Thirteenth Amendment, abolishing slavery, takes effect. Red Cloud, an Oglala Indian chief, leads Sioux warriors to halt the construction of the Powder River Road in Montana. The first luxury sleeping cars, designed by George Pullman, appear in the U.S.

1866 The Fourteenth Amendment, prohibiting voting discrimination, denying government office to certain Civil War rebels, and repudiating Confederate war debts, is passed. During Fetterman Massacre a U.S. army detachment of more than 80 is ambushed and totally wiped out by the Indians under Chief High Backbone in northern Wyoming. Alfred Nobel invents dynamite. Edgar Degas begins to paint ballet scenes. Western half of the Indian Territory (Oklahoma) is ceded to the U.S.

1867 Nebraska becomes a U.S. state. Alaska is sold to the U.S. by Russia for $7.2 million. The British North America Act establishes the Dominion of Canada. Gold is discovered in Wyoming. By the Treaty of Medicine Lodge, the southern Cheyenne Indians are assigned a reservation in Oklahoma. Diamonds are discovered in South Africa. Livingston explores the Congo. The Paris World's Fair introduces Japanese art to the West.

1868 Washita Indians battle in northern Oklahoma. Second Treaty of Fort Laramie grants Sioux Indians exclusive possession of the area in South Dakota, west of the Missouri River. Alabama, Arkansas, Florida, Louisiana, North Carolina, and South Carolina are readmitted to the Union after the Civil War.

1869 General Ulysses S. Grant is inaugurated as U.S. president. Woman suffrage law passes in the Territory of Wyoming. First population census is taken in Argentina. Suez Canal is opened. Mahatma Gandhi, Indian nationalist leader, is born (died 1948); first American Indian — Brigadier General Ely Samuel Parker — is appointed as Indian Affairs Commissioner (served till 1871).

1870 Women enter the University of Michigan, Ann Arbor, for the first time since its founding in 1817. Congress appropriates the first funds for the federally administered education in Indian schools. Hudson's Bay Company's northern territories are sold to the Canadian government. The First Ghost Dance Movement starts in Nevada.

1871 Congress terminates the use of Indian treaties, and Indians are thereafter governed by congressional legislation and executive agreements. Great Fire destroys Chicago. Trade unions are legalized in Great Britain. Older Joseph dies.

1872 The Modoc War (1872-73) between U.S. army and Modoc Indians, about the Indians' refusal to settle on Klamath Reservation in Oregon, ends with the hanging of tribal leaders. First U.S. national park—Yellowstone in Wyoming—is established.

1873 Major General George Crook successfully drives most Arizona Apache Indians onto reservations. First U.S. postal card is issued. First railroad reaches North Dakota, bringing many homesteaders. President Ulysses S. Grant formally establishes the Wallowa Valley as a reservation. A council is held at Lapwai between Nez Perce tribe and the superintendent of Indian affairs; Nez Perce are ordered once again to move to Lapwai Reservation.

1874 Gold is discovered on the Sioux Reservation; miners rush in. Adobe Walls Indian battle in northern Texas. The first American zoo is established in Philadelphia.

1875 England purchases Suez Canal shares. Rebellion begins in Cuba. A civil rights act gives blacks equal rights in public places, though school integration is not included; Supreme Court declares the act invalid in 1883. U.S. government reverses its position and declares the Wallowa Valley open to white settlement; the Valley of the Winding Waters becomes known as Union County.

1876 Colorado becomes a U.S. state. Ponca Indians are moved from Dakota Territory to the Indian Territory in Oklahoma, where one-third of the tribe perishes under harsh climate and scarcity of food. The Sioux Indian uprisings reach their peak when Chief Sitting Bull massacres Custer's troops at Little Bighorn in Montana. Secretary of War William Belknap is impeached for taking bribes for the sale of trading posts in Indian Territory. The Indian Act is passed by the Dominion Parliament in Canada, recognizing the government's responsibility for health, education, and welfare of Indians. Alexander Graham Bell patents the telephone. Mark Twain publishes *The Adventures of Tom Sawyer.*

1877 General Oliver Howard gives the Non-treaty Nez Perce 30 days to relocate; refusal of Nez Perce Indians to relocate leads to the Nez Perce War in which 239 Indians die and the U.S. looses 266 persons. For five months a band of about 300 Nez Perce warriors under Chief Joseph hold off a U.S. force of 5,000 troops. The Non-treaty Nez Perce are ordered to resettle from Wallowa Valley to Lapwai Reservation in Idaho. General Howard's troops are defeated by Chief Joseph's band at the Battle of White Bird Canyon; some 220 Nez Perce are killed at the Battle of Big Hole. Ollokot (brother of Chief Joseph), Chief Looking Glass, Chief Pile of Clouds, and Chief Tuhulhutsut are killed at the Battle of Bear Paw, Montana. Chief Joseph surrenders to General Nelson A. Miles; some 100 Nez Perce escape the surrender and join Chief Sitting Bull in Canada. Many of Chief Joseph's people die of malaria and other diseases at Fort Leavenworth, Kansas. Rutherford B. Hayes is declared the winner of 1876 presidential elections. Reconstruction of the South ends. Government gives Sioux Indians all Ponca lands in Dakota and Nebraska. After discovery of gold on their land, the Sioux Indians relinquished their land, and the "Great Dakota Boom" begins (1879). Indian Chief Crazy Horse is killed following his surrender.

1878 As the result of Bannock War, Bannock Indians are forced to return to their reservation in Idaho. Congress appropriates the first funds for Indian police forces. Chief Joseph meets President Hayes and pleads for the return of his tribe to their homeland in Oregon; his appeal is denied. Nez Perce are moved to Ponca Reservation. Thomas Edison invents the incandescent electric lamp.

1879 Ponca leader, Chief Standing Bear, and a group of his people return from their reservation to Dakota without permission where they are arrested and put into prison. In a landmark decision, *United States ex.rel. Standing Bear vs. Crook*, Ponca Chief Standing Bear and his loyal friends are freed from prison. A large number of Indians are killed in an attempt by Chief Dull Knife and his band to escape an Oklahoma reservation and return to their northern homeland. Construction of the Panama Canal begins. First American Indian school of prominence is opened with 147 students in Carlisle, Pennsylvania.

1880 A bill is passed in the Congress restoring land at Niobrora (Nebraska) to Ponca Indians. James Garfield is elected president. France annexes Tahiti. Department of Indian Affairs is established in Canada. Geronimo escapes from reservation in Arizona, but is brought back under Indian agent's custody.

1881 President Garfield is assassinated; Vice-president Chester A. Arthur becomes president. Helen Hunt Jackson's *A Century of Dishonor* about mistreatment of Indians is published. Indian Shaker church is formed in the state of Washington. Sioux and Cheyenne resistance ends with the surrender of Sioux Chief Sitting Bull.

1882 New York City installs first electric street lamps. U.S. bans Chinese immigration for the next ten years. A world exhibition opens in Moscow, Russia. American Baseball Association is found.

1883 World's first skyscraper, ten-stories high, is built in Chicago. New York's Brooklyn Bridge is opened. The Orient Express, traveling from Paris, France, to Istanbul, Turkey, makes its first run.

1884 France presents the Statue of Liberty to the U.S. Grover Cleveland is elected president. Indian police force is established on 48 of the 60 agencies (reservations). The Dreamer Cult arises among Indians along the Columbia River.

1885 Almost unlimited power of the Indian police is curtailed by the Major Crimes Act of Congress. Chief Geronimo once again escapes from reservation but is finally captured by General Miles. President Grant dies. Louis Pasteur develops a rabies vaccine. Chief Joseph and 150 Nez Perce are sent to Colville Reservation in eastern Washington after several years at the Indian Territory of Oklahoma; some 120 Nez Perce are sent to Lapwai Reservation.

1886 Geronimo, the last Apache Indian leader, surrenders, thus ending the long and bloody Apache Wars of New Mexico and Arizona. Federation of Labor is founded. Canadian Pacific Railway is completed. Slavery is abolished in Cuba.

1887 The Dawes Severalty Act (General Allotment Act) is passed by the Congress, (later amended in 1891, 1906, and 1910); the act challenges the whole Indian reservation system; it grants citizenship to those Omaha Indians who took land allotments. Area under tribal landholdings totals 138 million acres (reduced to 47 million acres by 1934). The first regulatory commission of the U.S., the Interstate Commerce Commission, is established.

1888 Benjamin Harrison is elected president. Sioux Indians suffer great loss as herds of their cattle are killed by blizzards and diseases.

1889 Montana, North Dakota, South Dakota, and Washington become U.S. states. Oklahoma is opened to non-Indian white settlement. United States Congress passes a law dividing the Sioux territory into six small reservations. The first run for homesteading by non-Indian settlers takes place in Oklahoma. Epidemics sweep through the Pine Ridge Indian Reservation. Chief Joseph sits for a bas-relief portrait in Portland, Oregon. Barnum and Bailey's circus opens in London.

1890 The last major conflict between Indians and U.S. troops, the Battle of Wounded Knee, takes place in South Dakota; 153 Sioux are killed and 44 wounded. For the first time U.S. census records Native Americans. The Second Ghost Dance Movement starts—also in Nevada. Daughters of the American Revolution (DAR) is founded in Washington, D.C. Japan holds its first general elections. Influenza epidemics flare up around the world. The Ghost Dance begins to take a strong hold among the Sioux Indians.

1891 Earthquake in Japan kills 10,000 people. Famine sweeps Russia. Trans-Siberian railroad construction begins. Dutch anthropologist Eugene Dubois discovers *Pithecanthropus erectus* (Java Man) in Java.

1892 Grover Cleveland is elected president.

1893 The World's Columbian Exposition opens in Chicago. Henry Ford builds his first automobile. Cherokee Outlet run for homesteading by non-Indian settlers in Oklahoma. France acquires protectorate over Laos.

1894 Charles Eastman, an Indian doctor, starts establishing Indian YMCA groups (some 40 between 1894-97). Korea and Japan declare war on China. Hawaii becomes a republic following a *coup d'etat*. Uganda becomes a British protectorate.

1895 Chinese are defeated in war with Japan. Cuba begins fighting Spain for independence. King C. Gillette invents the safety razor. Armenians are massacred in Turkey.

1896 Utah becomes a U.S. state. William McKinley is elected president. Mary Church Terrell helps found the National Association of Colored Women. Klondike Gold Rush begins in Alaska.

1897 William McKinley is inaugurated as U.S. president. Chief Joseph takes part in the dedication ceremony of the tomb for Ulysses Grant in Riverside Park, New York. First U.S. subway line opens in Boston. Severe famine hits India. Slavery is abolished in Zanzibar.

1898 U.S. annexes independent republic of Hawaii. Spanish-American War begins, and ends in Treaty of Paris. U.S. acquires the Philippines, Puerto Rico, and Guam. Cuba gains independence from Spain.

1899 There are about 225 day schools and 148 federally managed boarding schools for Indians, attended by some 20,000 Indian children.

1900 William McKinley is reelected president. Bubonic plague epidemic breaks out in the U.S. Australian Commonwealth is proclaimed. Carry Nation, a Kansas anti-saloon agitator, begins raiding saloons with a hatchet.

1901 President McKinley is assassinated; Theodore Roosevelt becomes president. First Nobel Prizes are awarded from a fund given by Alfred Nobel, inventor of dynamite.

1902 Cuba becomes an independent republic. Aswan Dam opens in Egypt. U.S. acquires perpetual control over Panama Canal.

1903 President Theodore Roosevelt appoints a commission to revise Sioux allotments so that all Indians should receive a fair share of the funds and can protect their title to land (result of Dawes Act). Orville and Wilbur Wright fly the first airplane at Kitty Hawk, North Carolina. Settlement of Alaskan frontier begins. Once again Chief Joseph goes to Washington to plead with President Theodore Roosevelt to grant his tribe the Wallowa Valley—their ancestral homeland; once again his request is denied.

1904 Theodore Roosevelt is elected to a second presidential term. Russia declares war on Japan. First railroad tunnel under North River between Manhattan and New Jersey is opened. Deaf and blind Helen Keller is graduated from Radcliffe College. Chief Joseph dies of a broken heart, away from his beloved homeland, on Colville Indian Reservation, Nespelem, Washington.

91; description of, 48-49; and
Indian reservation mandate, 14;
meeting with Chief Joseph
(Young), 48-50, 74; meeting with
non-treaty chiefs, 48-50; pursuit
of Chief Joseph (Young) by, 71-88
Hudson Bay Trading Company, 22,
25
Hush-hush-kewt, Chief, 48
Hutchins, Charles, 40
Idaho Territory, 24, 31, 73
Imnaha Valley, 48
Indian Reservation: Colville, 94;
establishment of, 32-36; Howard's
mandate on move to, 14; inspection
of, by non-treaty chiefs, 49-50;
Lapwai, 15, 44, 91, 94; Nez Perce,
11, 15, 35, 94; Ponca, 93
Isapsis-ilpilp, father of, 17
Jackson, Captain, 72
Jacobs, Lieutenant, 80
Jefferson, Thomas, 21
Jerome, Lieutenant, 87
Jones, John, 63
Joseph, Chief (Old); conversion to
Christianity, 24-25; remarriage of,
in Christian religion, 25; children
of, 26, 32, 30; relations with
Spalding, 28; retaking of Indian
name, 28; at Walla Council, 32-36;
and Treaty of 1855, 35; and Treaty
of 1863, 41; death of, 43; funeral
of, 43-44; wives of, 43
Joseph, Chief (Young): decision to
leave homeland, 11-12, 49-50; wives
of, 13, 61, 65, 81, 89; baptism of, 26;
upbringing of, 29-30; siblings of, 30;
entrance into manhood, 30; Indian
name, 31; criticism of white
government, 38; marriage of, 41-42;
description of, 42, 48; at Lapwai
Council (1873), 44; decision to fight,
51; preparation for war, 60-62;
children of, 61, 65, 86-87, 89; tactical
skills of, 65-70, 84-85; alliance with
new Chief Looking Glass, 68;
pursuit of, by General Howard,
71-75; meeting with General
Howard, 74; attempt to escape to

Canada, 75-80; negotiations with
Miles, 87-88; surrender of, 88;
interview with Rutherford B.
Hayes, 93; portrait of, 94; notoriety
of, 94-95; death of, 95; burial of,
95; distribution of property, 96
Joseph, Chief (Young) (illustrations):
2, 4, 8, 10; at dedication of Grant's
Tomb in 1897, **56;** medallion of, **57;**
funeral of, **57, 90;** monument at
Nespelem, Washington, **90, 97, 98**
Judith Mountains, 85
Kamiah, 50, 73
Kamiah Ferry, 73
Kamiakin, Chief, 32
Klickitat Indians, 32
land cession, in treaty of 1863, 41
Lapwai, 65; 1842 Council at, 25; 1873
Council at, 44; mission at, 24
Lapwai Creek, 24
Lapwai Reservation, 15, 44, 88, 91, 94
Lapwai Valley, 49
Lawyer, Chief, 44; and mining
operations on Indian territory, 39;
role of, in treaty of 1855, 34-36; **52**
Lewis, Meriwether, 21, 22
Lewiston, 65; establishment of, 39-40
Little Rockies, 86
Little Salmon River, 61
lodges, 22
Lolo Trail, 21, 46, 73
Looking Glass, Chief (Old), 48
Looking Glass, Chief (Young), 49, 50,
71, 77, 79, 81; alliance with Chief
Joseph (Young), 68; cavalry attack
on, 67-68; daughter of, 81; death of,
87; peace attempts by, 76
malaria epidemic, 92
measles outbreak, among Cayuse
Indians, 27
medicine men, 15
Miles, Colonel/General, 86, 88, 91;
negotiations with Chief Joseph
(Young), 87
Miles City, 91
Mill Creek, 33
Miller, Marcus, 65
mining operations, on Indian
territory, 39

missionaries: De Smet, Father, 24;
Spalding, Henry and Elisa, 24;
Whitman, Marcus, 27
Missoula, 76, 79
Missouri River, 85, 86, 92
Montana, 31, 46, 61
Montieth, Agent, 46, 47, 50
Mount Idaho, 59, 65, 68
Musselshell Creek, 86
Nespelem, Washington, 94
Nez Perce Indians: dwellings of, 22;
criminal law system for, 25;
decision to leave Wallowa Valley,
11-18; fighting style of, 64; foods of,
19, 24; French naming of, 22;
governing structure for, 25-26;
history of, 19-28; loss of ancestral
land, 41; and mining operations on
land of, 39-40; non-treaty tribes, 40,
41, 42, 46; origin legend of, 20;
passage into adulthood ceremony,
30-31; Pikunanmu tribe of, 15;
religion of, 24, 26-28, 29-30;
reservation land of, 11, 15, 35, 94;
tribal customs of, 25, 29-31; tribal
homeland of, 11; tribal name of, 19;
Wal-lam-wat-kin band of, 12
Nez Perce War (1877), 59-87; broken
agreements after, 91-95; Indians'
decision to enter, 51; marker in
Oregon showing where it started,
55; surrender of Indians, 87-89
Nimipu Indians. *See* Nez Perce
Indians
Norton, Mr., 60
Norton farm and stagecoach station,
59, 68
Odeneal, T. B., 44-45
Old Blackfoot, 62
Ollokot, 26, 29, 30, 32, 50, 61-62, 65;
death of, 87; description of, 48;
meeting with General Howard,
47-48
Oregon, 19, 27, 31, 66, 91
Oregon Territory of, 11;
establishment of, 31-32; U.S. claim
to, 31
Oregon Trail, 23
Oro Fino Creek, 39

Ott, Larry, 17
Palmer, General, 28
Pandosy, Father, 33
Pen-pen-hi-hi. *See* White Bird, Chief
Perce, establishment of, 39-40
Perry, David, 68, 69; at Battle of
White Bird Canyon, 60-63, 65
Peu-peu-mox-mox Indians, 36
Pierce, Elias D., 39
Pile of Clouds, 77; death of, 87
polygamy, 29-30
Ponca Reservation, 93
Presbyterian religion, 24
Puget Sound, 37
Rabbit Skin Leggins, 23
Rains, Lieutenant, 69
Rawn, Captain, 79
Red Wolf, Josiah, **55**
religion, 45; Dreamer faith, 15, 42,
43, 48; and the Great Spirit, 29, 30;
Indians' interest in whites, 23;
introduction of Christianity, 23-28;
Spirit Chief, 16, 21, 31; of treaty
versus non-treaty Indians, 43
right of discovery, 31
River Crow Indians, 85
Rocky Canyon, 15
Roosevelt, Theodore, 95
Ruby Creek, 79
Saint Mary's Mission, 24
Salmon River, 11, 15, 19, 48, 51, 61,
67, 77
Salmon River Valley, 66
Salt Fork River, 92
Second Cavalry, 87
settlers, conflicts between whites,
and Indians, 27, 32-38
Seven Devils country, 66
Seventh Cavalry, 84
Shoshone Indians, 82
Simpson, Sargeant, 69
Sioux Indians, 86
Sitting Bull, Chief, 85-86, 87, 88, 89
Slate Creek, 17
Slaterville, establishment of, 40
Smohalla, 41
Snake River, 13-15, 19, 39, 40, 48, 66
Spalding, Elisa, missionary work by,
24; **53**

108

Spalding, Henry; looting of home, 27; missionary work of, 24, 26-27, 29; relationship with Chief Joseph (Old), 24-25, 28; **53**
Spirit Chief, 16, 21, 31
Stevens, Hazard, 33
Stevens, Isaac, role of, in establishing Indian reservation, 32-36
Stevensville, 77
Stevens War, 37-38
Stinking Water River, 84
Sturgis, Samuel D., 84, 85, 87
Sweetwater Creek, 49
Tewats, 15, 48; war position of, 18
Timothy. *See* Twisted Hair, Chief
Tongue River, 91
Trail Creek, 79
Treaty of 1855, 48; Chief Joseph's (Old) refusal to sign, 35; provisions of, 34-35; signing of, 35-36
Treaty of 1863, land cession by Indians in, 41
treaty tribes, 40, 59, 88; religion of non-treaty versus, 43
Treaty War, 37-38
Trimble, 64
Tu-eka-kas, Chief. *See* Joseph, Chief (Old)
Tuhulhutsut, Chief, 15, 48, 49, 50, 65; death of, 87; religion of, 15, 16
Twisted Hair, Chief, 21; conversion to Christianity, 24, 25, **52**
Umatilla Indians, 33, 47; reservation land of, 35
Um-til-ilp-cown, 17
Union County, 46
United States, 1846 treaty between Great Britain and, 31
Valley of Winding Waters. *See* Wallowa Valley
Walaitits, 18; father's murder, 16-17
Walla, council at, 32-36
Wal-lam-wat-kin Indians, 40, 42; land claims of, 48

Walla Walla, 27
Walla Walla Indians, 33, 36; reservation land of, 35
Wallowa Range, 19
Wallowa Valley, 11, 42, 46, 48, 66, 95; opening of, to white settlement, 46; soldier occupation of, 50; and Treaty of 1863, 41
Warner, Olin, 94
War of 1812, 22
Washington Territory, 31-32
Weippe Prairie, 1874 meeting at, 46
We-tot-yah, 47
Whipple, Stephen, 68, 69
Whisk-tasket, Chief, 41
White, Elijah, 25
White Bird, Chief, 59, 60, 65, 77, 79, 91; in battle of Big Hole, 81; decision to fight whites, 16, 18, 49; escape to Canada, 89; selection of reservation land, 50; Indian name for, 48
White Bird Canyon, 61, 66; battle at, 61-64
White Cloud, Chief, 82
White Pelican. *See* White Bird, Chief
white superiority myth, Indians' acceptance of, 23
Whitman, Marcus, 27
Whitman, Narcissa, 27
Wieppe Prairie, 21
Wilkinson, Lieutenant, 49
Wood, Colonel C.E.S., 94
Wood, Erskine, **56;** visit with Chief Joseph (Young), 94
Wright, Colonel George, 38
Wyoming, 31
Yakima Indians, 32, 33, 37
Yellow Bull, **52,** 65, 87
Yellowstone Park, 83, 84
Yellowstone River, 91

ABOUT THE AUTHOR

Mary Virginia Fox was graduated from Northwestern University in Evanston, Illinois, and now lives near Madison, Wisconsin, located across the lake from the state capitol and the University of Wisconsin. She is the author of more than two dozen books for young adults and has had a number of articles published in adult publications.

Mrs. Fox and her husband have lived overseas for several months at a time and enjoy traveling. She considers herself a professional writer and an amateur artist.

FRANKLIN PIERCE COLLEGE LIBRARY

00081627

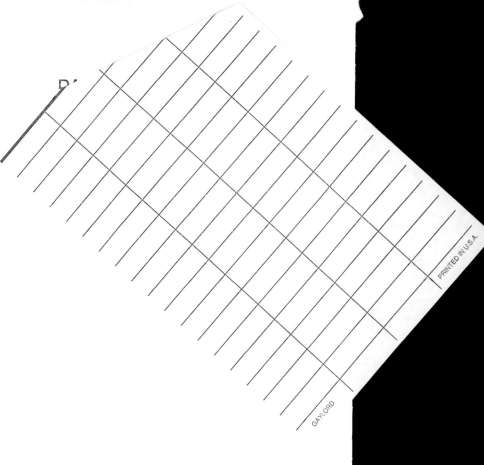

D'

ABOUT THE AUTHOR

Mary Virginia Fox was graduated from Northwestern University in Evanston, Illinois, and now lives near Madison, Wisconsin, located across the lake from the state capitol and the University of Wisconsin. She is the author of more than two dozen books for young adults and has had a number of articles published in adult publications.

Mrs. Fox and her husband have lived overseas for several months at a time and enjoy traveling. She considers herself a professional writer and an amateur artist.

FRANKLIN PIERCE COLLEGE LIBRARY

00081627